BUDGETING

FOR BEGINNERS

Cut Your Expenses in Half and Double Your
Income

(Easy Tips to Set Up an Easy Budget and Start
Saving Your Money Now)

Robert Crook

Published by Alex Howard

Robert Crook

All Rights Reserved

Budgeting for Beginners: Cut Your Expenses in Half and Double Your Income (Easy Tips to Set Up an Easy Budget and Start Saving Your Money Now)

ISBN 978-1-77485-061-9

Legal & Disclaimer

Table of Contents

Introduction

In this book, we are going to look into what budgeting is. There is usually a big misconception when it comes to the term budgeting, which many think of as depriving themselves of the things they'll miss, however, it needn't be all like this. Many turn the other away, completely in denial of managing their resources, giving in to their spending habits when all that is needed is to make some simple adjustments to how they spend their money.

Going back to the true definition of the word budgeting, we see that it means not living beyond your means, whether that is in the present or the future. A plan is needed, along with a great deal of discipline in setting a budget for any outgoing funds. This can be comparable to a dieter who needs to choose which foods to eat, instead of not eating much of anything at all.

The term "budgeting" or "budget" may make you feel uncomfortable to use as a word. Nevertheless, you can always use a different one if you prefer. For example, you may call it something like "my money plan "or "my financial strategy," which is another way of calling it a budget. It's a great way to take the initiative in organizing your finances.

It's no wonder that financially successful people have their plan, or budget, at hand and carefully look at every penny they spend. Ultimately, this is the key to their monetary success. A budget can be set for a great number of reasons which are not just limited to those who lack disposable income. It is common for people to set budgets for retirement, buying that new house or for a down payment, to even a wedding. With the latter, you may now better understand why people do set a budget. The straightforward answer to this is simply that they know what is happening with their money and they can have greater peace of mind because they are in complete control of their finances at all times. The good news is that setting a budget is a straightforward matter, regardless of how little or high your income is. In principle, what you are doing is building awareness on how you use your money, nothing more and nothing less.

This book is the ultimate resource for managing your finances more efficiently so you can improve your spending habits to the point where you'll see a significant difference. No matter if you are a student, a family person, business tycoon or a retiree.

I congratulate you for taking the first step in setting a budget. Your best financial friend will be your budget. It's a tool that you'll use to keep your finances in shape; therefore, you will also learn here how to not only design one but to keep it evergreen. I also cover problematic areas such as what to do if you have not stuck to your budget or, for whatever reason, if your circumstances change. However, you use this book, you can go back to it time and time again as a reference to help guide you through your budgeting success.

Chapter 1: Budgeting 101

Budgeting is a task most people are never taught to do. Looking at income and expenditures is not fun, particularly if you are feeling a little guilt for overspending.

Before we take a look at what has happened in the past, take a moment to be kind to yourself. Forgive yourself for mistakes you have made in the past and congratulate yourself on these bold steps you are taking to give yourself and your family financial peace of mind.

Ready? Let's begin budgeting!

The first thing to do is write down everything you spent last month. It may not be easy, but do your best. The point is to get a good idea of where your money is going so that you can start to make adjustments.

Once you have written down where you spent your money, you are going to take a good hard look at the different categories you spend in and determine what you can cut back on and what you can eliminate. Below are some tips to help you determine a workable budget for yourself.

First, a word of warning. When determining your budget please be realistic! If you are too strict in your budget, you will wind up sabotaging your efforts. You have to still enjoy life, so make sure there is a little money set aside for entertainment and fun. This will help you stick to your budget.

Make sure you analyze where you are spending money, particularly on non-necessary items. What can you cut out or substitute with a more budget-friendly option? Often, restaurants and bars fall into this category. Try having friends over instead of going out, you'll save quite a lot of money. Instead of sending your children out to the movies, rent a movie (or better yet, get one from the library) and make pizza at home.

Some guidelines for where to spend money are: 50% on fixed costs, 20% on your long term financial goals and 30% on flexible spending.

Fixed costs are things that don't vary from month to month, like mortgage or rent payments, car payments and utilities. Other things that fall into this category that could be temporarily cut out include gym memberships, online accounts like Netflix or Gamefly and magazine subscriptions. Try to drive this budgeting category to below 50% and put everything you save toward debt repayment.

Long term financial goals are the savings and investments that will secure your financial future. The three pillars here are paying down debt, saving for retirement and building an emergency fund. We'll talk more about an emergency fund in a later chapter. Once you are out of debt, you can also include larger items, like a down payment on a house or saving for a new car. I strongly suggest automating your savings so that you never have the opportunity to spend the money. You can investigate programs like Digit and SmartyPig to see which works best for you.

Finally, flexible spending is the day to day expenses that you will be able to cut down to the bone. These include eating out, buying new clothes, hobbies, groceries and other entertainment. While groceries are a necessity, there is a lot of flexibility in what you purchase. You can spend a lot to purchase already made meals or you can spend much less and cook from scratch. The less you spend here, the faster your debt will be paid down.

Your goal in the budgeting phase is to cut out as much as possible while still being realistic about how much you must spend. It's a balancing act and may take a month or two to get right. As long as you start off by making every minimum payment and funding your emergency fund, you will be on the right track. With each month, you can make further refinements to your process.

Chapter 2: What Is Budget Management?

What Is a Budget?

A budget is an estimation of sales and prices over a designated future time and is generally compiled and re-evaluated on a periodic foundation. Budgets may be made for a person, a family, a group of humans, a business, a central authority, a country, a multinational agency or just about whatever else that makes and spends money. At corporations and businesses, a budget is an internal tool used by management and is frequently now not required for reporting using external parties.

What is budget management?

The optional module budget control enhances and expands your finances improvement capabilities inside well-known Ledger. Budget management permits you to:

Create multiple 'what if' scenarios for making plans purposes and to degree the impact of change.

Budget for both projects and debts

Create your budget using modern-day or any preceding years' finances information.

Replica a budget from any other year, fast manipulate finances up or down the usage of amounts or percentages, and use an unlimited wide variety of finances distribution tables.

Define one account's budget as a percent of every other's price range.

Enter information into a notepad of the way the finances for a particular account became advanced.

Document budget changes and documents in your original or adjusted budget.

Venture last actual amounts primarily based on year-to-12 months consequences and the once a year budget

The budget—for planning and control

Money and time are scarce assets to all people and groups; the efficient and effective use of those assets requires planning. Planning by myself, but, is inadequate. Control is likewise vital to make sure that plans simply are achieved. A budget is a device that managers use to devise and manipulate using scarce assets. A budget is a plan displaying the organization's goals and the way control intends to collect and use sources to acquire one's objectives.

Organizations, nonprofit companies, and governmental gadgets use many one-of-a-kind forms of budgets. Obligation budgets are designed to choose the overall performance of an individual section or manager. Capital budgets compare lengthy-time period capital initiatives including the addition of device or the relocation of a plant. This bankruptcy examines the master price range, which consists of deliberate running finance and an economical price range. The deliberate running budget helps to devise future profits and results in a projected income declaration. The financial budget enables management to plan the financing of belongings and effects in a projected stability sheet.

The budgeting system involves making plans for destiny profitability due to the fact incomes an affordable return on sources used is the number one enterprise objective. A company ought to devise some techniques to deal with the uncertainty of the future. An enterprise that does no making plans by any means chooses to deal with destiny via default and might react to activities simplest as they arise. Most groups, but, devise a blueprint for the movements they may take given the foreseeable events that can arise.

Businesses can use budget-to-real comparisons to evaluate character overall performance. For instance, the same old variable value of manufacturing a personal financial laptop at IBM is a budget determined. This parent may be as compared with the real value of producing personal computer systems to help examine the overall performance of the personal laptop production managers and personnel who produce private computers. We can do that type of evaluation in a later bankruptcy.

Many different blessings result from the preparation and use of budgets. As an example: groups can better coordinate their activities; managers emerge as aware about other managers' plans; employees become greater fee aware and try to preserve sources; the organization evaluations its company plan and modifications it while important, and managers foster an imaginative and prescient that otherwise might not be advanced.

The planning process that effects proper finances offers a possibility for various stages of control to think via and devote destiny plans to writing. Also, a nicely prepared budget allows management to comply with the management-with the aid of-exception principle via devoting interest to outcomes that deviate substantially from planned degrees. For most of these reasons, a budget should honestly mirror the expected consequences.

Failing to finances because of the uncertainty of destiny is a terrible excuse for no longer budgeting. The less stable the situations, the more essential and perfect is budgeting, although the manner will become extra difficult. Solid operating situations allow more reliance on beyond revel in as a basis for budgeting. Recall, however, that budgets contain more than an organization's beyond effects. Budgets additionally do not forget a company's destiny plans and express predicted activities. As a result, budgeted overall performance is greater beneficial than past performance as a basis for judging actual consequences.

A budget needs to describe management's assumptions referring to the nation of the economy over the planning horizon; plans for adding, deleting, or converting product strains; (3) the nature of the enterprise's competition; and the results of current or viable authorities guidelines.

Budgets are quantitative plans for the future. But, they may be primarily based in particular on past enjoy adjusted for destiny expectations. For that reason, accounting records associated with the past play a critical element in budget education. The accounting gadget and the budget are intently related. The details of the finances should believe the corporation's ledger accounts. In flip, the accounts ought to be designed to provide the ideal information for preparing the budget, monetary statements, and period in-between economic reports to facilitate operational management.

Control ought to regularly compare accounting facts with budgeted projections for the duration of the length of the finance and look into any differences. Budgeting, but, is not a substitute for good management. As an alternative, finance is a vital device of managerial management. Managers make decisions in finances preparation that function as a course of action.

The period included by using a budget varies in line with the character of the unique activity concerned. Cash budgets may additionally cowl a week or a month; sales and production budgets may cover a month, a quarter, or a year; and the general working finances may additionally cowl a quarter or 12 months.

Budgeting includes the coordination of financial and nonfinancial planning to fulfill organizational desires and goals. No foolproof method exists for preparing a powerful budget. However, finances makers ought to carefully bear in mind the situations that follow:

Top control helps all control degrees should be aware of the finance's significance to the corporation and must realize that the budget has pinnacle control's assist. Top management, then,

16

has to absolutely nation long-range dreams and extensive goals. Those goals and targets need to be communicated during the organization. Long-range goals include the anticipated quality of services or products, growth fees in sales and earnings, and percent-of-marketplace targets. Overemphasis at the mechanics of the budgeting process has to be avoided.

Participation in intention setting management makes use of budgets to expose how it intends to accumulate and use assets to attain the company's lengthy-variety desires. Employees are much more likely to try in the direction of organizational desires if they take part in placing them and in making ready budgets. Frequently, personnel has sizeable information that would assist in getting ready a meaningful budget. Also, employees can be motivated to carry out their capabilities within finances constraints if they are dedicated to reaching organizational goals.

Speaking results humans have to be right away and sincerely knowledgeable of their progress. Effective conversation implies timeliness, affordable accuracy, and stepped forward information. Managers have to efficiently communicate outcomes so employees can make any vital modifications to their overall performance.

Flexibility If massive primary assumptions underlying the budget trade in the course of the yr, the deliberate operating finances should be restated. For manage functions, after the actual stage of operations is thought, the real revenues and prices may be in comparison to anticipated performance at that stage of operations.

Observe-up budget follow-up and statistics feedback are a part of the manipulate aspect of budgetary control. Because the budgets are dealing with projections and estimates for destiny operating effects and financial positions, managers should constantly test their budgets and correct them if vital. Often management makes use of performance reports as an observe-up tool to compare actual outcomes with budgeted effects.

The period budget has poor connotations for many employees. Frequently within the past, management has imposed finances from the top without considering the opinions and emotions of the employees affected. This type of dictatorial technique can also bring about resistance to finances. Some of the reasons may underlie such resistance, consisting of lack of expertise of the procedure, concern for fame, and an expectation of multiplied pressure to carry out. Personnel may agree that the performance evaluation technique is unfair or that the desires are unrealistic and inconceivable. They will lack self-assurance inside the manner accounting figures are generated or can also decide upon a much less formal verbal exchange and assessment gadget. Regularly those fears are unfounded, however, if personnel agree with those troubles exist, it's miles hard to accomplish the targets of budgeting.

Issues encountered with such imposed budgets have led accountants and management to adopt participatory budgeting. Participatory budgeting manner that every one range of control responsible for real performance actively takes part in placing operating dreams for the approaching duration. Managers and different personnel are much more likely to understand, be given, and pursue goals while they are involved in formulating them.

Inside a participatory budgeting method, accountants need to be compilers or coordinators of the price range, not preparers. They have to be on hand for the duration of the preparation process to present and give an explanation for vast financial records. Accountants must pick out the relevant cost data that enables management's objectives to be quantified in greenbacks. Accountants are chargeable for designing meaningful budget reviews.

Also, accountants need to always try to make the accounting system extra attentive to managerial needs. That responsiveness, in flip, will increase self-assurance within the accounting gadget.

Even though many corporations have used participatory budgeting efficaciously, it does now not usually paintings. Studies have proven that during many groups, participation within the finances formulation didn't make personnel greater motivated to obtain budgeted goals. Whether or now not participation works rely upon on management's leadership style, the attitudes of employees, and the corporation's size and shape. Participation is not the solution to all the issues of budget education. But, it is one way to acquire higher results in businesses that might be receptive to the philosophy of participation.

Budget Management Tips for New Managers

When a worker is promoted to his or her first control role, this will probably be the primary time he or she manages a branch price range.

Most new managers acquire little or no formal education in a way to increase a budget forecast, tune their costs, or how to make mid-yr changes. They may be frequently surpassed a spreadsheet or report from their manager, or the finance branch, and predicted to know the way to do it or analyze by using trial and error.

While "trial and blunders" can be a powerful way to study a new skill, it would be higher if a new manager didn't need to make too many painful mistakes. Here are a few suggestions if you have been promoted as a supervisor with a budgeting duty.

Make investments the Time to analyze properly from the start

There may be no higher time to invite "silly" questions than while you are present-day to something and feature by no means finished it. Better ask and spend the time upfront in getting to know, than wait until a person has to factor out your mistakes. Request time from your supervisor (or predecessor if you may) to study the underlying philosophy, the overarching dreams, the layout, and each line item. If your organization has a finance character, ask that individual to spend time with you as well. Maximum can be flattered and willing to percentage their understanding. In any case, if they could educate you on a way to do things according to their specs prematurely, you'll be much less of a headache for them later on.

Take a "Finance and Budgeting for Non-financial Managers" path

Take a look at together with your neighborhood college enterprise colleges, below "executive education." maximum business colleges offer one- to 3-day, non-credit guides. Throughout or after the direction, make the effort to review your company's annual document and recognize the numerous financial ratios and reports.

Manipulate your department finances like it's Your very own business

While we work for big organizations, we tend to deal with "the organization's" money as though it grows on bushes. It doesn't, and it's now your job as a supervisor to take private ownership of your department's assets.

Be a team participant

If feasible, evaluate your supervisor's price range. While it's crucial to take ownership of your price range, your unit is part of a larger entity. Ask your manager to show you where your budget suits and supports the large photograph in addition to the interdependencies together with your friends. There may be times while any other department needs money for goals that are a higher priority than yours. Don't wait to be requested or have it taken away—be proactive and offer to help your peer manager. You will be seen as strategic and collaborative.

Don't play silly games

Just due to the fact "everybody does it" doesn't mean it's no longer stupid and terrible for the employer. An example of an average stupid budgeting game that managers play is "use-it or lose-it spending." it is while you are becoming near the cease of the year, and your budget is running underneath your forecast. In preceding years, while you underspent, your next year's budget became set based totally on that year's real. So, in order now not to have your budget cut once more, you cross on a shopping spree—buying belongings you don't want or stocking up if you would possibly want it.

Tune your expenses month-to-month and Make Proactive Corrections

Don't anticipate that "a person" will inform you while you are over budget. In reality, you possibly even ought to ask for month-to-month reports or maintain a song yourself. Don't wait until the quilt of the yr, when it will become a surprise to you and your boss. Via then, it's too past due to analyze and make corrections. Be responsible, measure yourself, and proactively record in your supervisor.

Be transparent and contain Your crew

Percentage your budget together with your crew, possibly even getting them involved in putting in place the forecast. Regarding your crew and supporting them recognize the budgeting manner creates an experience of shared possession and encourages your employees to locate creative methods to manage charges.

Be Strategic

Don't just take the final 12 month's actuals and upload 10 percent to the subsequent 12 month's forecast. Begin with growing a method and dreams, then determine the sources required to attain one's goals. If you require more than closing yr, prepare a business case to justify your request for extra funding.

Don't Overdo It

While handling the budget is a crucial function for a supervisor, never lose sight of the maximum crucial belongings: your humans! Make certain you're spending at least five instances the quantity of time growing your team than crunching numbers.

What is the importance of budgeting?

Considering budgeting allows you to create a spending plan in your money, it ensures that you may constantly have sufficient money for the things you need and the things that are critical to you. Following finances or spending plans will also preserve you out of debt or help you work your manner out of debt if you are presently in debt.

A budget is a plan that suggests all of your month-to-month coins inflows and outflows. It's miles a snapshot of what you have and what you anticipate/plan to spend, which allows you to reap your economic goals, through helping you pick out your spending and saving habits.

Why is budgeting important?

Budgeting is the most crucial part of financial planning. The amount of cash absolutely everyone has isn't a sign of ways a lot of cash they make but rather how effective their budgeting is. If you need to deal with your finances efficiently, you want to recognize where your money goes. Opposite to how it can appear, budgeting isn't always hard, it is not complex, and it does now not reduce the amusing out of your lifestyles – budgeting saves you from destiny economic hardship and a life of debt.

A way to create a price range

You may use a clean sheet of paper or a spreadsheet on a laptop to increase your finances or use the template underneath.

That will help you fill out your template and apprehend your money conduct, you may go through the relaxation of the module.

How a whole lot of cash do you are making?

Do you earn your income weekly, bi-weekly, or monthly?

Your finances need to anticipate the identical time table as the general public of your charges, which tends to be month-to-month. Calculate how an awful lot of money you make after taxes and consist of all possible income, (ex. Income, recommendations, bonus, and so on.). If you handiest work seasonally, then average out your profits to last you the whole year, in 365 days.

Know wherein your money is going

What are your prices? Remember the fact that understanding where your cash goes always keeps you on top of things of your finances. Recall your constant prices and variable charges.

Constant expenses are expenses which might be usually the equal quantity every month. What are your fixed prices?

Variable prices are your abnormal fees; they're charges which you have manage over. What are your variable charges?

A way to hold music of your charges

Music costs, preserve each receipt, or take pics of each receipt and make a separate folder for it to your phone

Sign up in online banking so the entirety is recorded for you

Assess your bank and credit card statements carefully each month – banks could make mistakes too!

General your charges at the cease of each month and assess how you're spending your cash

This cash should always be stored or invested. If the difference between your profits and expenses is poor, that means you're spending more than you're incomes. You ought to decrease or cast off some of your fees.

Write some approaches you may store in the dreams phase of your personal financial budget within the template, earlier than you cross directly to the next module.

Great blessings of Budgeting Your cash

Budgeting is the maximum elementary and basic tool for coping with your cash. Nonetheless, a considerable majority of human beings avoid having a budget as its "more paintings". Regularly time human beings agree with that budgeting additionally dictates that you are no longer allowed to have amusing and enjoy matters. Allow me to inform you from over a decade of budgeting that is false, surely, it does the exact opposite.

What budgeting virtually accomplishes is it genuinely suggests you the way to allocate your money. It offers you in-depth expertise of what you can manage to pay for to spend your money on and knowing your financial limitations. Budgeting will prevent the grief of overspending and the probable reason you to climb into greater debt, something a lot of us battle with.

There are so many advantages to budgeting. One in every one of my favorites is it does no longer prevent you from playing the things you locate happiness from in lifestyles. It truly does the alternative and allows you the freedom of doing more of the matters you like.

The benefits of Budgeting:

1) Provides you one hundred% control Over Your money

Consider this for a 2d. If you aren't controlling your money, is it controlling you?

Finance is a savvy manner of intentionally controlling your money. Budgeting permits you to live with far less strain without having to fear approximately those unexpected expenses that arise (way too regularly I'd upload). It also permits you to understand where your spending habits are weakest.

Each day cup of espresso can truly add up over time. According to ABC information the common American spends close to $1, one hundred according to year on coffee alone. Budgeting will help you decide if giving up your morning cup of espresso is well worth the financial savings to position closer to some other place like paying off debt or saving in your subsequent own family holiday.

2) Permit's you tune your monetary desires

Another gain of budgeting your cash is helping you avoid spending on needless expenses, services, and merchandise which might be cutting into your financial goals. If you have set earnings budgeting will assist you to make ends meet a whole lot easier each month without all of the stress.

Sit down and write out your monetary goals. Once you have them written down on paper and you take control of your money it's lots much less probable no longer to satisfy them.

3) Budgeting Will Open Your Eyes

Budgeting lets in you to recognize exactly in which your money is coming from, in which it's miles being spent, and what kind of you've got on the cease of every month. This provides you with entire expertise in your price range.

A budget lets in you to apprehend what you could have the funds for, make the most of buying and making investment

34

possibilities and plan for a way to lower your debt. It also suggests to you what's vital to you based on wherein you spend your money in the course of the month. This can help you regulate your spending behavior inside the proper course to reach your goals.

4) Will help organize Your Spending

When starting to finances, begin via breaking down all your costs for the month consisting of cable, the internet, loan, coverage, groceries, amusement, eating place, health club memberships. Printing a budget template will help you stay organized.

This makes it smooth to quickly view exactly how much you are spending on your character offerings each month. Another purpose to break these down into classes it's miles permits you to look if a bill is going up with a company. Currently, our garbage invoice turned into raised by using $10 a month. Budgeting allowed us to see this alteration speedy so I used to be able to name and get our invoice returned to the authentic charge.

We've got used Mint for nearly a decade for monitoring our month-to-month prices. It's truly unfastened to sign up and they make budgeting extremely green.

5) Will help create a Cushion for surprising fees

A trip to the hospital, automobile repairs and plumbing trouble are all unexpected prices that arise on occasion. It is vital which you have money set apart for these kinds of occasions, aka an emergency fund.

The final issue you would need to do is not have enough money to cover the charges and have to rate it to a credit score card which you have already got running stability on.

6) Budgeting Makes Talking About Finances Much Easier

Approximately budgeting your parents, girlfriend, boyfriend, or partner can be difficult on occasion. A few may also say it's even "taboo" (that is ridiculous).

Having a budget permits you to have a cold tough data when it comes to speaking. This makes having a calm Communication about money a good deal less complicated.

The budget is the most common argument between a married couple's palms down. One of the most important benefits of budgeting is reducing the general pressure surrounding the "money conversations".

Talk in your extensive different and get on the same web page. Open and honest conversation continually wins in marriage. Set aside a "discretionary class" for your price range, this permits for you each to have a restriction however also allows you to spend the money the way you need to (makeup, Amazon, eBay, myth soccer, video games, protein, and so on).

7) Having a budget allows you to shop a "safety internet"

While trouble arises in life like unemployment you will be geared up. I am hoping this never happens to you, but budgeting will let you be organized if it does.

Having a protection net will preserve you afloat if your profits stop coming in. The pronouncing goes "have sufficient in your protection net to last up to six months with no profits".

Without our safety net, I might probably have by no means been capable of stopping my job and start running a blog complete-time. Agree with me having a safety internet will open up doorways! You will in no way feel trapped again.

8) Allows You to Pay down Debt fast

Going to school, eliminating a mortgage, and buying a new car are a few methods we people go into debt. Know-how your debt is extraordinarily critical! Making sure you understand your hobby rates, terms, and duration of loans will be crucial in controlling your debt.

Budgeting will give you a clear know-how of how to pay down your debt. You may discover that you can without problems start to cut in other regions so you can afford to make greater bills for your debt.

9) Budgeting facilitates You invest

Investing is an extremely good way to have your cash be just right for you. Contributing to your retirement early and regularly must be for your radar so you can retire as deliberate.

A few people use the rule of "whatever is left on the give up of the month I'm able to put in my retirement". This is a backward questioning attempt converting your mind-set to "paying yourself first". Meaning understanding how a lot you want to position away for retirement and paying yourself before something else. Manifestly, this takes time to learn how to balance it effectively so all of your bills nonetheless get paid however this is by far the quality way to reach your funding/savings dreams.

10) Last, but Not Least it allows you to Live Life Better

Living Frugal and free

We've said this earlier than and could preserve to say it till someone proves to us in any other case. Controlling your money will have a big advantageous effect on your life!

We have a passion for budgeting and with Mint it takes us much less than 10 minutes in step with month to test our budget.

Brittany and that I believe fabric matters only offer you a brief small portion of happiness. You get to enjoy them for a little while, but that fades very quickly. We're all about reports and creating lifelong reminiscences collectively!

Budgeting has enabled us to have one hundred% to manipulate our money. Allowing us to travel extra, begin our blogging commercial enterprise, end my process, spend more time with our families, and a lot greater!

If beginning finances interest you with pen and paper we created a budgeting binder only for you. Easy input your email copes within the container under and we can send it directly on your email to get started.

Motives why you want a Budgeting

If you've heard it as soon as, you've heard it 1000 instances: finance YOUR money! Monetary professionals and cash advisors were shouting this mantra from the mountaintops for years.

That is just one of these financial training that cannot be preached enough. If you and your own family need monetary security, following a budget is the simplest answer.

1. It facilitates you maintain Your Eye at the Prize

Finance allows you to figure out your long-time period goals and work toward them. If you waft aimlessly through life, tossing your money at every pretty, brilliant object that occurs to seize your eye, how can you ever store up enough money to buy a vehicle, take that trip to Aruba, or placed a down price on a residence?

A finance forces you to map out your goals, shop your cash, hold track of your development, and make your goals a truth. Adequate, so it could harm while you recognize that today's Xbox game or the fantastic cashmere sweater in the store window would not suit your budget. However, when you remind yourself which you're saving up for a new house, it will likely be a whole lot easier to show around and stroll out of the store empty-surpassed.

2. It helps make certain you do not Spend money You do not Have

A way too many clients spend money they do not have—and we owe all of it to credit cards. As a count number of fact, the median credit score card debt in step with family reached $2, three hundred in June 2019.

Earlier than the age of plastic, human beings tended to realize if they were dwelling inside their way. At the end of the month, if they had sufficient money left to pay the bills and sock some away in financial savings, they were heading in the right direction. In recent times, people who overuse and abuse credit playing cards do not usually recognize they may be overspending until they may be drowning in debt.

But, if you create and stick to a finance, you'll never discover yourself in this precarious position. You will know precisely how plenty of cash you earn, how a whole lot you can afford to spend each month and what kind of you want to save. Certain, crunching numbers and preserving the tune of a finance is not nearly as a lot of fun as happening a shameless shopping spree. However take a look at it this manner: when your spend-satisfied friends are making an appointment with a debt counselor this time subsequent year, you will be jetting off for that adventure you've been saving for—or higher yet, stepping into your new home.

3 It allows result in a Happier Retirement

Shall we embrace you spend your money responsibly, follow your finances to a T, and in no way bring credit card debt. Precise for you! However, are not you forgetting something? As critical as it's far to spend your cash accurately today, saving is also crucial in your destiny.

Finances can help you do simply that. It's vital to build investment contributions into your price range. If you set aside a portion of your income every month to make contributions to your IRA, 401(k) or different retirement funds, you will sooner or later build a pleasing nest egg. Even though you can need to sacrifice a bit now, it will likely be worth it down the street. In any case, might you as a substitute spend your retirement golfing and taking trips to the beach or working as a greeter on the neighborhood grocery shop to make ends meet?

4. It allows you put together for Emergencies

Life is filled with surprises, a few higher than others. While you get laid off, turn out to be ill or injured, go through a divorce, or have a loss of life within the own family, it can result in a few critical economic turmoils. Of route, it looks as if these emergencies continually rise on the worst feasible time—while you're already strapped for coins. That is precisely why every person wishes an emergency fund.

Your finances ought to encompass an emergency fund that includes at least three to six months' worth of living expenses. This more money will make sure which you don't spiral into the depths of debt after a lifestyle disaster. Of path, it's going to take time to save up three to 6 months' well worth of residing expenses.

Don't try to unload the general public of your paycheck into your emergency fund properly away. Build it into your price range, set realistic dreams and begin small. Even if you placed $10 to $30 aside each week, your emergency fund will slowly build up.

5. It enables Shed light on awful Spending habits

Constructing a finance forces you to take a close study of your spending conduct. You can be aware that you're spending cash on belongings you do not want. Do you watch all 500 channels to your highly-priced extended cable plan? Do you need 30 pairs of black footwear? Budgeting permits you to rethink your spending habits and re-focus your monetary dreams.

6. It's Better Than Counting Sheep

Following finances will even help you capture more close-eye. What number of nights have you ever tossed and turned stressful approximately how you had been going to pay the bills? Folks that lose sleep over monetary issues are allowing their cash to control them. While you finance your money wisely, you may never lose sleep over economic problems again

Chapter 3: Living Paycheck To Paycheck

Are you tired of the constant feeling that you don't have any money? Living paycheck to paycheck is a real problem for many people. While some of the people in this rut are low earning families, many are not. Those in the middle class can also become entrenched in this cycle.

There is an old saying that you will spend what you earn. Generally it is expected that you are living within your means and meeting all of your financial obligations. At the same time, you don't have any money left over. As you earn more money you take on additional expenses or luxuries that eat up the additional income. This is how many families fall into the paycheck to paycheck cycle.

It is very possible to break this cycle. You have to have some willpower. You have to force yourself to deal with delayed gratification. Here are some tips for breaking the cycle.

The Importance of Curbing Spending

Most people who have trouble making ends meet or running out of money before the next paycheck hits actually spend quite a bit on unnecessary expenses. When you cut back on some of the luxuries of life you will find that you can save vast amounts of money. Even if it is something as simple as choosing an off brand at the grocery store, all of those pennies and dollars add up quickly. Here are a few ways you can curb your spending.

1.Limit fast food trips to two per month

2.Buy off brands at the grocery store

3.Shop thrift stores for clothing before going to department stores

4.Limit entertainment such as movies and concerts to one per month

5.Cut out or cut down your cable or satellite bill

6.Cut back on cell phone usage and bills

7.Never use payday loans—they cost more than they're worth

8.Cut back on driving to the bare minimum to save on gas

9.Turn up the thermostat in the summer and down in the winter—dress for the weather instead of compensating with high energy bills

10.Cut out or cut back on vices such as soda and cigarettes

11.Make your own desserts instead of buying prepackaged cookies and cakes

These are just some of the ways you can trim the fat from your spending. Carefully consider where you spend money that you don't need to spend. Anything you can cut back would be beneficial. At the same time, don't deny yourself every pleasure. You have to feel like you are benefiting from your frugal lifestyle and all of your hard work. Denying yourself every luxury all the time will cause you to give up on budgeting.

The Importance of Saving for the Future

One of the biggest problems with living paycheck to paycheck is that you don't save back any money for the future. Whether you are looking five years ahead or thirty, it is important to save at least a small amount from each paycheck toward your long term goals.

Of course, the big savings goal many people think about is their retirement. If you are younger than 40, this event may seem so far in the future that it is hardly worth worrying about. However, this is the attitude that is leaving many middle aged adults struggling to figure out what they are going to do when they have to retire. Saving money for your retirement needs to start at a younger age. If you start early, you can save a large amount of money without hurting your average income and spending.

There are many other things that are closer to the present that you might want to save up for. If you are close to any of these events, or you just want to be prepared for them in the future, you should definitely start saving now. Here are just a few.

•A wedding for yourself or your child

•Preparing for a baby

•College tuition for a child

•A car that you don't have to make payments on

•A down payment on a house that will save you on housing costs

•A nest egg for maintenance or replacement of major appliances as they age

•A family vacation that your children will remember for a lifetime

Saving money isn't just about surviving. It's about living. Without saving back money for the little things, and the big things, that come along in life, you will fail to truly enjoy them when they arrive because you will be struggling to pay for them. Planning ahead not only keeps you prepared for emergencies, but also decreases stress and increases overall happiness.

How Budgeting Helps You Meet Your Goals

Budgeting is an important step in helping you meet your goals. Budgeting isn't just about being careful with your money. You can use budgeting tools to help you plan your income and spending so that you can intentionally set aside savings. You can use expense tracking to help you trim the fat from your budget and see where you can make changes to improve your overall quality of life, now and in the future. Your long term financial goals, as well as your short term way of life, can only be realized through effective budgeting.

Methods of Budgeting

There are three primary ways to budget. You can budget by week or pay period, month, or by expense. Budgeting by expense is the easiest way to budget. It is generally done by using the envelope method, which will be explained shortly. Budgeting by week or pay period can help you stop the paycheck to paycheck cycle, but works with that mentality while you work to improve your financial habits. Monthly budgeting is helpful because you can see everything you spend monthly at one time. This is important because many bills are only paid once per month.

You may choose to use a combination of methods. Sometimes it can be helpful to have even the most basic monthly budget to use in combination with a weekly budget. It can also help to use the envelope method, especially if you have difficulty setting aside money for larger expenses.

Chapter 4: Follow The Money

There is a saying that failing to plan is planning to fail. If you can't see where you're going, how can you get there? The biggest corporations in the world plan and create budgets to track their finances. As a matter of fact, any company, big or small, that is serious about success will have a budgeting process.

Many people are scared to budget because of two main reasons. First, they think it's a complicated process, and second, they say that it's a time consuming task that isn't worth doing. Some probably even work for companies that have entire departments tasked with just doing budgets, and the prospects of doing the activity on their own seem downright intimidating.

Well, you're going to learn how to do one in a matter of minutes, so buckle up.

Basic terminologies and concepts

Before we get to the how-to, understand that your budget is a PLAN that lays out your future activities in terms of dollars and cents. You will actually be watching your financial "life" unfold before you. Best of all, you now have the power to control your finances, where they used to control you.

Every budget has two components, money that you take in, or earn (**income**), and money that you put out (**expenses**).

What the budgeting process aims to accomplish are,

(1) Make sure that at the end of each month, we have income left over for savings, by

(2) Controlling, and monitoring your expenses.

Expenses are further broken down into either **fixed** or **variable** expenses. The difference is important for budgeting your future expenses. A **fixed expense** is money that you spend every month no matter what. It doesn't change regardless of what you do. These are expenses that you do not have any power to control, at least in the short term, and they have to be paid no matter what.

The following are fixed expenses that you will need to track:

Rent

Mortgage payments

Car loan payments

Tuition/day care/babysitting

Student loan payments

Other fixed loan payments, such as installment payments on lines of credit or appliances and furniture

Tax installment payments

Credit card payments (more on this later on!)

Utility bills – While electric, gas, water, and phone bills do change every month, y0u know that you will need to pay them. These will include bills for pest control and gardening work that you contract out.

Insurance premiums (health, life, and vehicle insurance,)

Property taxes

Children's lessons and activities

Note that some of the above expenses, while fixed, are not necessarily paid monthly. Many tax bills are paid quarterly, semiannually, or annually. Health insurance premiums are also paid quarterly most of the time. You will need to consider as we go along.

Variable expenses are money that you can elect to spend, or choose how much to spend. This includes practically everything else that you spend that is not otherwise classified above as a fixed expense.

Variable expenses typically include the following:

Groceries

Personal care items including medicines

Gasoline/Fuel

Tolls and parking

Clothing

Work lunches, coffee, & snacks

Eating out

Entertainment (movies, shows, spectator sports)

Tobacco / alcohol

Out of pocket medical expenses

Public transportation (bus, trains, etc.)

Gambling and lottery

Magazines / newspapers / books (regularly scheduled subscriptions may be classified as fixed)

Haircuts/ beauty salon treatment and services

Religious/church contributions/tithes

As a general rule, if you don't know where to classify an expense item, it is a variable expense. If you have infrequent or miniscule expenses for certain things like printer ink cartridges, and parking and tolls, for example, can be grouped with supplies, and transportation or automobile expenses, respectively.

Collect and organize your records

Now we get to the fun part. Actually doing the budget! The first thing you need to do is collect all the pay slips and other documents that support the income you received. This may include bank statements for interest you receive on deposits, and direct deposits of salaries, commissions, and bonuses.

Most of the work involved in this process is assembling bank statements, credit card statements, bills, receipts, and every piece of paper and document to support the items that you have paid for. You might also want to print out any emails that support your financial transactions, such as an acknowledgement of a payment that you made.

For our purposes, you will need to collect at least three months worth of information.

From your credit card, bank statements (from using your ATM cards), PayPal statements or any summaries that you get containing information on expenses, mark each item that represents outgoing cash flows for any type of expenditure that you have incurred.

The reason you need to do this is you need to establish a historical basis for planning your income and expenses. Laying out what you have done in the past is essential in planning your future.

Next, you need to group the documents into three groups, or piles, if you will:

The income pile,

The fixed expense pile,

The variable expense pile.

Once you are confident that you have all the information available, you can now use the spreadsheet tool in the next chapter to capture the expenses.

Chapter 5: What Is Budgeting?

I'm Sure you hear this "budgeting" term all the time, but it is important you truly understand what it is and its importance. To give you a better understanding it is completely necessary we take a look at budgeting—specifically what the term means. It is in your best interest to further clarify what "budgeting" means because this term is often misunderstood.

For instance, in popular culture, when someone says that a particular item is not in their budget, we assume they mean they can't afford it. The word 'budget' is confused with money, precisely how much you have and what you can afford. It is not strange that people would think this way. After all, we hear a lot about institutions having big budgets or running over budget. Like "the school has a big budget" or "local government is running on a stringent budget." We assume this means they have a lot of money or no money at all. Granted, you might not be wrong in thinking this. It may very well be what people mean. But this is not what the term 'budget' refers to.

Budgets are about controlling and monitoring how you spend money over a specific period. It is both a prediction and a plan. It predicts how much money you will have and what your expenses are going to be. And it plans how you will divide your money, usually with the goal of avoiding financial troubles like unnecessary debt. A budget also monitors where your money goes; no cent goes unaccounted for. It is a three-pronged attack: predict, track, and plan.

From the onset, we can see that it isn't about what you can afford or how much money you have, but it can inform your spending. It might be that a local municipality with a big budget is in debt or a school with a stringent budget has a lot of money. Although it is rare, it can happen, those two things are related but not in a way that people think.

Budgets are about making your goals a reality. This is not the only reason they are useful (We will talk more about the benefits of budgeting in the next chapter.) We know budgets help us in our goals because we often hear people talk about budgeting for x or z. People might say "I am budgeting for a new phone," or "I am budgeting for a new car." This means the budget plan they follow drives them towards a new phone or car. This usage of the term is correct, but it has a bad connotation like budgeting is not fun; later, I will convince you otherwise.

This technique is often used by businesses, governments, and wealthy people to manage their finances. This fact makes some people think budgeting is a luxury, that if they live paycheck to paycheck budgeting is not for them. But this is not true. Budgeting is beneficial to everyone, and I hope you can begin to see why this is so. While the goal of many budgets is to save money, budgets are also about spending wisely and avoiding financial troubles. I am a big believer in using your budget to do all these things.

In the next chapter, I talk about the importance of budgeting. You might think I already have, but there is much more to learn.

Chapter 6: Budgeting Basics

It can be said that the hardest part about living on a budget is sticking to it. We always have the best of intentions when we create a personal or household budget but is "actually following the budget" that is the most difficult part of the whole situation. However, I would argue that forming the habit is the difficult part. After that habit is formed, it can be fairly easy to stick to it.

We don't all know what "living on a budget" entails. When you hear that phrase, what do you instantly think of?

"Having no fun."

"Saving all of your money."

Is that about right?

Create Some Goals

We are all in different parts of our lives. Because of this, we all have different financial obligations. Not only that, but we also want different things out of our futures.

Some of us want to be able to retire and travel. Some just want to be able to live in a tiny house. Other people want to be able to have vacations homes that they can visit when they feel the urge to move around. Some of us need to save for our families. Others just want some play money and money to live comfortably in the future.

Ask yourself what you want out of your life. What kinds of short term and long term goals do you have and how do you need to financially ready yourself for those goals? Keep in mind that short terms goals should take no longer than a year to complete while an example of a long-term goal would be, "Save for retirement" or "Put away money for my child's education."

Do you need to save a lot of money for a new house? To be ready for children? Or perhaps so you can start your own business. How long will it take for you to save up the necessary funds to make these goals attainable?

Remember that these goals aren't set in stone. Things happen in our lives that make us rethink what we want out of our future. You can change the items on this list as you grow older and experience more things.

Pay Close Attention To Your Net Income

One of the biggest pitfalls when it comes to planning out and living on a budget is creating and following a plan that is within your income. In a time where material possessions have become something of a status symbol, we have learned to live outside our means. This is one of the main reasons why a lot of people are in credit card debt and can't stick to a budget or save money.

The first step that you identify how much money you have coming in. Knowing your income is important. Some of you may have to estimate how much you have coming in every month because you own your own business, run a freelance or by-contract business, or because your income fluctuates.

If this is you, make sure that you underestimate how much income you bring in each month. I only suggest this because it is easy to overestimate and that will cause your budget to be unreasonable and unattainable.

Also remember to take into account your employer deductions for taxes, retirement plan, insurance, Social Security, and maybe spending account allocations.

When You Create Your Plan

When you create your budget plan - and you've found your average monthly income – divide your income into two big categories: fixed spending and variable expenses.

The expenses that would fit under fixed spending would include your utilities and bills that don't change much each month. This would include your mortgage, car payments, credit card payments, regular utilities, etc.

The items that would fit under variable expenses include expenses that change every month: entertainment, food (though this can fit in either depending on your habits), gas and travel expenses, etc.

I suggest that you record these expenses for a couple months to see what your trends and habits fall. If you are anxious to get a budget plan ready, I suggest that you look into your bank records. Online banking has made things incredibly easy these days. Some online banking accounts even break down your spending for you depending on where you shop.

My online bank account does that exact thing; they organize my spending habits by categories. This makes it much easier to keep track of where my money goes.

At the minimum, I would manually break up your spending into three different categories:

Needs and necessities

Savings

Desires

Needs include the fixed and variable costs that are necessary to living a healthy life. The savings section would include both emergency funds and retirement. The desires section would cover everything else.

Now it is time to personalize your budget.

Okay, so you've analyzed your spending habits. Now it's time to personalize a budget. A great thing that is simultaneously obnoxious is the fact that every budget should be personalized. This means that you don't have to be pigeonholed into keeping a budget that doesn't fit your needs (Yay!). However, this also means that you have to work harder to come up with the perfect budget that does (Ooh…).

Okay, now that you've figured out what your fixed spending number is, set that aside every month so that you will always have that money available for important expenses. What you have left should be divided up into variable items. This number is also a variable in and of itself. If you allow a certain amount of things like clothes, but you know that you need to save for a TV, you can skim a little from your clothes fund and add that to your TV fund.

Making Your Budget.

Creating your actual budget can be done in as little as four steps after you've done all of that prep work.

Keep a record of your spending and analyze your results. Record your spending and have your significant another record theirs as well. I suggest keeping a small notebook and pen with you at all times for one month. In addition to that, keep a spreadsheet on your computer. Transcribe your.

Plan for your next month's spending. If you live with a significant other, make sure that you plan together and that you take all of your expenses into consideration, even if you both have separate bank accounts. You don't have to keep track of each other's "desired" sections. However, it is important to come up with a spending cap. When you want to buy something of a certain amount – which will differ with each couple – you may want to defer with each other. Some of you may not need to do this. Others feel that it is a courtesy to one another. While others yet feel that it is necessary because you have joint accounts. My husband and I keep our own records for little spending. However, if something costs $100 or more, we mention it to each other. If something costs $500 or more, we discuss it as a team so that we can come up with rational and smart choices.

Look for ways that you can spend less. While spending a little bit for a long time can add up, so can saving a lot of money. Saving just a little bit over a long period can add up to some incredible savings. To do this, consider some of these options:

1) Shop at a cheaper grocery store

2) Buy generic brands

3) Cook at home instead of eating out

4) Entertain at your house instead of going out to a club or movie

5) Utilize coupons during sales

You can also find ways to boost your income. If you have a hobby or talent, you may be able to use it to earn some extra money. Teaching your hobby to others can prove to be profitable. You can also sell your wares on an online shop, or at local markets. One great bonus is that you may be able to turn this side job into a full-time job if you ever lose your main source of income. Handy, huh?

Check Your Spending Habits On A Monthly Basis

Are you sticking to your budget? If not, where are you going astray and how can you fix that? Take a look at your spending every month and compare it to your budget worksheet to see how things are going. If you find that you're often going over-budget in some areas out of necessity, you should consider cutting elsewhere to keep things under control.

Chapter 7: Brain Hack - The Psychology Of Bargain Shopping

Black Friday, which is the Friday after thanksgiving, is a bargain hunter holiday. It signals the start of the holiday shopping season where bargains are the "it thing" across the west but especially in the United States. Let us be truthful for a minute; no one hates a bargain. If you ask Warren Buffet, the billionaire, he will say that if you can get the same quality goods or services at a cheap price, the cheaper option is best. To simplify it, bargain hunting is the art of searching for bargains. There are a million and one reasons why we search for bargains but central to all these reasons is to save some money. The thrill of bargain hunting is also something that most of us find very exhilarating. Imagine grabbing a $200 coat or item for less that the retail price. Would that not be great?

Bargain hunting may seem like a narrow street with well lit up ads and streetlights. However, this is not so especially because of the mental component of bargain shopping. This may sound like something a psychiatrist would say, but I will explain myself in a minute.

Your brain networks in a very specific way at the prospect of a discount. Some experts have gone as far as to state that bargains create a sort of dumb blindness in even the most rational shopper. I can attest to this. When you see a bargain or what is often times made to look like a bargain (I am talking about those 40% off ads and posters across the supermarket or online store), your body reacts by sending some endorphins into your brain, then the "bargain adrenaline." Within no time, you are strolling down the supermarket dragging a "crap laden" stroller cleverly disguised as bargains.

Supermarkets and major stores are the Albert Einstein's of getting money out of your pocket. They are multinationals looking to take every penny they can out of your pocket which means, they will hire the best and employ the best tactics just to make you to spend some more money in their stores, but can you blame them? You are the whole reason they are in business. One of the most common mind tricks that these consumer-driven multinationals and chain stores use is something very simple but powerful beyond words: If you place a chosen (carefully so) cheap item in a buyer's clear sight of vision, chances are, they will buy it.

Here is something you probably did not know. Most of the items labelled as bargains in the store are probably the items that will earn the store the most money after sale. This means that if you do not check your bargain shopping mindset, you will only end up with "non-bargains" and adding dollars to the chain stores' bank accounts. All of us are suckers for targeted bargains mental cues; this is rightly described in Ellen Ruppel Shell book

"Cheap: the high cost of discount culture" and is something that the godfathers of American discounts, Wanamaker and Woolworth exploited to their advantage. It is also the root cause of retail holidays such as pre and post black Friday, black Friday, Christmas, Clearance etc. What is the correct frame of mind when shopping for discounts?

The Correct Bargain Shopping Mindset

This also sounds like something a psychiatrist or yoga expert would say, "You need to tune out the 40% discounts to get to the real discount". Nothing rings truer that this statement. Remember what I said above; stores are clever, and they will do everything they can to milk every penny out of you. Discount shopping is one of the strategies they employ. Therefore, while you may be looking for a bargain, you may not be getting a bargain.

Preparing your mind is critical to finding a bargain. I realize that this also sounds very vague and something someone who has never experienced the thrill of a bargain hunt would say. However, remember the endorphins and shopping adrenaline we talked about earlier; they only serve one purpose, which is to excite and confuse you. Stores rely on this.

To prepare yourself mentally, you need to open your mind to every possibility, including not finding that bargain. You need to come to the realization and the decision that, not every labelled bargain is in fact a bargain. You also need to come to the fact that, if you do it correctly (without the over excitement), more often than not, you will walk into a store offering bargains and walk out without buying anything because there is no value for money.

Additionally, you should also change the way you look at shopping and more precisely, bargain shopping. As earlier stated, not everything with the discount label is a bargain. In fact, most bargains are often time not labelled. With this in mind, and a changed mindset, you will be able to navigate the "bargain murky waters" with ease.

Now that we have looked at some of the tricks that stores will use to get you to buy "non-bargain bargain labelled" items, and seen the correct mindset to employ when shopping for bargains, let us look at some other tips you can use to get the best out of your bargain-shopping trip.

Chapter 8: Why Should I Have A Budget?

What is a budget?

A budget is an estimate of your income and expenses for a specific period of time. Budgets can be weekly, monthly, quarterly, or annually. We use budgets to help us keep track of what we spend versus what we save; and oftentimes our budgets help us successfully plan for things like retirement and purchasing a home. A budget is one of the main tools used by successful entrepreneurs.

Is budgeting right for you?

If you are an individual dealing with money on a daily basis, having a budget is beneficial to you. Who doesn't deal with money nowadays? With a nicely formed budget, you will understand your finances better and be able to take control your impulses.

When is it necessary to have a budget?

A budget is necessary the moment you start earning money and accumulating expenses. Watching your expenditures in light of your income, and how it affects your bottom line, is definitely a skill that every individual needs to learn.

What you do with it matters.

What you do with a budget is very crucial to the success of that budget. Some people treat it like a wish list; they can make one and forget all about it once they're doing creating it. A budget needs to be paid attention to, if it's going to work. You will need to be dedicated to following it and tracking your performance over the timeframe you made it to cover.

Don't make excuses.

Do you think you don't have time to do a budget and track your performance? Using the excuse that you don't have time to do a budget only leads to financial ruin. Most people avoid budgeting because it requires them to actually look at their spending habits. We don't want to give up those impulse purchases we make. But, the next time we need money to buy a new car or take a vacation, we cannot do it because we did not budget. When we are honest with ourselves and do not make excuses about our financial choices, we find that a budget is the one thing we should have been doing all along.

In the society we live in today, we need to have a budget for the following reasons:

Companies want our money. At home and away, we see brands advertising everywhere. We see sales messages that try to explain the "benefits" of buying whatever product or service is being sold.

Impulse buying is too easy. Most of people get paid by the hour, and they work hard for their money. But, those companies who want our money have made it extra easy for us to make unplanned purchases by way of credit. This is why credit is so dangerous.

Because, as soon as we get into a store, we oftentimes don't consider the expenses we have at home. We think that if we put our impulses on credit, we will be able to afford what we want, now. But all this does is puts us deeper into debt, and causes us to give more money to these companies and banks who charge us interest. This is why we must learn to control ourselves and put our financial priorities in front of our "I want it now," spending habits.

Your dreams cost money. Your budget is your dream's best friend because it helps you avoid giving companies your money for unnecessary purchases. When you properly manage your finances, you are able to adequately fund your dreams. Research shows that writing down your tasks and goals increases the odds of you accomplishing them. So, start budgeting now!

How else does budgeting help you?

Mentally prepares you to reach your goals. Having a budget and looking at it daily will help you set mental reminders that act as roadblocks to unplanned spending.

Ensures that your money goes where it is needed most. We all know that spending money is very easy. A budget will not only set mental reminders for you, it will help you understand why you need to listen to those warnings, so you can avoid wasting money on your "greeds" and instead, you will spend it on your needs.

Helps you build true wealth. When budgeting becomes part of your daily habits, you will build wealth without much effort. But, budgets don't just affect your financial wealth, they also influence these other forms of wealth:

a) More time to do what you want with the people you love most.

b) Better health. Most of our stress is caused by financial issues. Studies have shown that stress increases our blood pressure, heart rate, bad eating habits, and the list goes.

c) Giving to the less fortunate. This is an underestimated area of wealth that many people forget about. Giving to those in need not only makes you feel good about yourself, it has also been proven to make others feel good too.

Prepares you for emergencies. Let's face it, unplanned emergencies is something most people don't think about. This is why so few people have life insurance or health insurance. Budgeting puts us in the position to be prepared for unexpected expenses that result from unforeseen curve balls that life might throw our way. It's always great when you don't have to borrow money to pay for unplanned emergencies.

Better understanding of your business. If you are an entrepreneur, then budgeting will help you better understand your business. How else will you know if you're making or losing money?

3 bad reasons to not budget.

You make a lot of money.

You think you can keep track of your expenses, mentally.

You never had a problem with money before.

3 reasons these are not good.

You make a lot of money. Not only does making a lot of money mean nothing, it is one of the main reasons people go broke when they lose their jobs. When your income is high, it is very easy to believe that you're safe from financial ruin. In fact, the opposite is true. Most people who earn a nice income from a job end up convincing themselves that their income is their safety net. So, they allow themselves to live beyond their means and spend money on things they cannot afford; in many cases buying things they don't even need with credit. Did you know that most high income earners are having financial difficulties?

You think you can keep track of your expenses mentally. Some people have the amazing ability to memorize things. Despite this fact, a great memory is not going to protect you against wild spending. There are tons of people who can memorize numbers, but without self-control over their finances, they still wind up in debt. The Harvard MBA Program discovered that writing down a task or a goal increases the odds of that task/goal being accomplished. For that reason, keeping a to-do list still remains one of the best ways to be productive and efficient.

You never had a problem with money before. Some people don't feel the need to budget because they might be against capitalism, or maybe they're just good at not spending money on things. But, many of these same people hoard the money they make and forget to enjoy some of it; like engaging in planned recreational activities like vacations. Depriving yourself of using the money you earn is not what budgeting is about. It is about helping you become more aware of how you can use money to reach various goals in life.

Just for the record: It is easier and better for someone to generate an extra income to save money, than it is to restrain yourself from spending in order to save. If you are looking to save a lot of money, a combination of managing and creating new sources of income is important.

FACT: Did you know the average millionaire has 7 streams of income?

Chapter 9: What Is Meaning Of Budget And Budgeting?

What is Budgeting? What is a Budget?

Planning is the way toward making an arrangement to go through your cash. This spending plan is known as a financial limit. Making this spending plan enables you to decide ahead of time whether you will have enough cash to do the things you have to do or might want to do.

What is planning? It is a significant arranging and determining procedure to assist you with dealing with your cash by offsetting your costs with your pay. Planning is basically offsetting your costs with your pay. On the off chance that they don't adjust and you spend more than you make, you will have an issue. Numerous individuals don't understand that they spend more than they acquire and gradually sink further into obligation consistently.

On the off chance that you need more cash to do all that you might want to do, at that point you can utilize this arranging procedure to organize your spending and spotlight your cash on the things that are generally essential to you.

Why is Budgeting so Important?

Since planning enables you to make a going through arrangement for your cash, it guarantees that you will consistently have enough cash for the things you need and the things that are critical to you. Following a financial limit or spending plan will likewise keep you out of obligation or assist you with working out of obligation on the off chance that you are at present in the red.

Shouldn't something be said about Budget Forecasting and Planning?

Steps To Build a Budget That Works

When you make your first spending plan, start to utilize it and get a decent vibe for how it can keep your accounts on track, you might need to outline your spending plan or spending plan for a half year to a year not far off. By doing this you can without much of a stretch estimate which months your accounts might be tight and which ones you'll have additional cash. You would then be able to search for approaches to try and out the highs and lows in your accounts with the goal that things can be progressively sensible and charming. Expanding your financial limit out into the future additionally enables you to conjecture how a lot of cash you will have the option to put something aside for significant things like your excursion, another vehicle, your first home or home redesigns, a crisis bank account or your retirement. Utilizing a reasonable spending plan to figure your going through for the year can truly assist you with your long haul monetary arranging. You would then be able to make reasonable suppositions about your yearly pay and cost and plan for long haul money related objectives like going into business, purchasing a speculation or diversion property or resigning.

In the broadest sense, a spending limit is a designation of cash for some reason. The word once used to signify "pocket" or "satchel"; a financial limit along these lines is "what's in the pocket." Budgeting as an action goes in degree from overseeing family funds on up to the arrangement of the Budget of the United States, attempted yearly by Congress; that archive is almost 1,400 pages long. This article will concentrate basically on "formal planning" as rehearsed in enterprises, here and there called the "spending process." Planning has consistently been a piece of the exercises of any business association of any size, however formal planning in its present structure, utilizing current planning disciplines, developed during the 1950s as the numerical supporting of corporate arranging. Current corporate arranging owes a lot to activities research and frameworks hypothesis. A pioneer in that field, Russell L. Ackoff worked intimately with General Electric, Anheuser-Busch, and other significant enterprises. His first book regarding the matter, the first of four, A Concept of Corporate Planning, had a significant effect.

Present day formal spending plans not just confine uses; they additionally foresee salary, benefits, and rates of profitability a year ahead. They have developed into instruments of control and are additionally utilized as a methods for deciding such awards as benefit sharing and rewards. Except if the budgetary procedure is made do with outrageous expertise and care, the very ethics of planning can transform into negatives—and have, generally, rose into a development effectively attempting to change this procedure.

Planning AS A PROCESS

In huge enterprises, planning is an aggregate procedure where working units set up their arrangements in similarity with corporate objectives distributed by top administration. Every unit plan is expected to add to the accomplishment of the corporate objectives. Unit supervisors get ready projections of offers, working costs, overhead expenses, and capital necessities. They figure working benefits and profits for the venture they expect to utilize. The spending itself is the projection of these qualities for the following schedule or monetary year. As a component of this procedure, every unit shows its arrangements and spending plan to an exploring upper administration board and May, from that point, roll out whatever improvements result from guidelines from or exchanges with the more elevated level. Writings displaying, archiving, and protecting the methods of reasoning fundamental the numbers are normally part of the arranging record. Endorsed spending plans at that point become the guide for activities in the coming year. In a perfect world month to month or quarterly spending audits track execution against the financial limit. As a component of such audits, changes to the monetary allowance might be affirmed. At year-end directors are made a decision by their presentation against the spending limit.

Numerous private ventures attempt to work without a conventional spending plan. Indeed, even a few organizations that have a spending only here and there counsel it, which means they are not picking up the business points of interest that they could be through planning. For startup business people, a financial limit resembles a guide that can assist them with defining objectives and survey the legitimacy of their business idea. For set up private ventures, a spending limit can be utilized to take the beat of the business, deciding how the business is performing as the years progressed, and distinguishing conceivable future speculations. By routinely counseling a financial limit, business pioneers can analyze genuine figures and catch potential business setbacks or different issues early. Spending plans can likewise be instrumental in prevailing upon speculators, persuading banks your business is a decent credit hazard, or expediting new accomplices or clients.

While spending plans are created base up, administrators must endeavor to meet top-down business objectives (e.g., "Yearly development in after-charge benefits of 39 percent."). Since execution is estimated dependent on meeting or surpassing positive projections (of offers, returns, and benefits) and meeting or coming in beneath negative projections (fixed and variable expenses and capital uses) chiefs have solid motivations for anticipating the most reduced conceivable "positive" and the most noteworthy conceivable "negative" results. The more effective they are in downplaying deals and benefits and overestimating costs, the higher the probability of "meeting the financial backing." Top administration's motivating forces, on the other hand, are to do the inverse. In this manner the planning procedure is naturally set apart by potential clash. Such troubles can be, and generally are, alleviated by balanced approaches, positive attitude on the two sides, and straight forward execution. Projections ought to be as sensible and quantifiable as could be expected under the circumstances. In the event that projections are off the mark with recorded examples, up or down, the executives must scrutinize the arranging. In this way, for example, a forcefully rising projection of costs must have some certifiable defense. Excessively aspiring income projections should likewise be addressed. Then again, chiefs must oppose pressures forcefully to raise income targets except if unmistakable changes in the market or repaying brings up in deals uses are available. On the off chance that the arranging levels are straightforward and sensible, the correct projections will result. In a perfect world, working units ought not be estimated on exercises over which they need full control. An activity which doesn't work its own obligation assortment, for instance, ought not be estimated on how quickly solicitations are gathered. Since spending plans are frequently at any rate 50 percent mystery, formal budgetary survey at sensible interims and practical changes dependent on genuine occasions must be a piece of a well-working procedure. Very frequently, the spring planning occasion is quickly overlooked.

Advantages AND COSTS

The absolute most potential advantage of formal planning lies in guaranteeing that capable directors require some serious energy every year (and afterward at fixed interims consistently) in contemplating their activity by taking a gander at all of its perspectives. Planning makes a complete image of things to come and makes the two chances and hindrances cognizant. This premonition at that point encourages direct everyday exercises. The central expense of the spending procedure is time. In certain organizations the procedure takes on its very own existence and turns into a tangled exercise of inordinate multifaceted nature which, in addition, keeps unit administrators from doing any reasoning: their time is expended in endeavors to agree to a huge range of prerequisites directed from above. A significant part of the negative frame of mind that has created concerning this action has its underlying foundations in superfluous bureaucratic inconveniences from one viewpoint and lack of quality in light of quick change a couple of months out.

Kinds OF BUDGETS

The two predominant types of planning are conventional and zero-based. Business arranging is typically a blend of the two. Customary planning depends on a survey of authentic execution and afterward the projection of such discoveries to the future with adjustments. In the event that swelling is high, for example, cost patterns of the most recent quite a while are anticipated forward however with alterations both for expansion and for anticipated development or decrease in business movement. Chronicled deals designs, utilizing built up patterns in deals development, are anticipated; new deals from arranged new item presentations are then included. Zero-based planning is the making of a totally new spending plan starting from the earliest stage—as though no history existed. When utilizing this strategy, the activity must legitimize and archive each thing of consumption and salary once again. Spic and span tasks will use zero-based strategies.

In government arranging, yet truth be told, infrequently in business, execution planning is utilized as a third other option. Under this technique, the monetary allowance is fixed at the start. The arranging action is to decide precisely what exercises will be done utilizing the allotted assets. Execution planning is now and again utilized in the corporate setting when the promoting spending plan is discretionarily set in that capacity and-such a percent to anticipated deals. The publicizing capacity at that point utilizes execution planning to allot the spending limit to different items and media.

For the independent company, various kinds of spending plans can be drafted to screen different monetary parts of the business.

• Operational spending plan - An operational spending plan is the most widely recognized sort of spending plan utilized. It figures and attempts to pretty intently foresee yearly income and costs for a business. This financial limit can be refreshed with genuine figures on a month to month premise and afterward you can amend your figures for the year, if necessary.

• Cash stream spending plan - An income spending subtleties the measure of money you gather and pay out. This is by and large counted on a month to month premise, yet a few organizations arrange this week after week. In this financial limit, you track your deals and different receivables from salary sources and difference those against the amount you pay to providers and in costs. A positive income is basic to develop your business.

• Capital spending plan - The capital spending encourages you make sense of how a lot of cash you have to set up new gear or systems to dispatch new items or increment creation or administrations. This spending gauges the estimation of capital buys you requirement for your business to develop and build incomes.

As ahead of schedule as 1992, the well known master of the board, Peter Drucker, wrote in The Wall Street Journal: "Vulnerability—in the economy, society, governmental issues—has gotten so incredible as to render worthless, if not counterproductive, the sort of arranging most organizations still work on: anticipating dependent on probabilities." Vulnerability has, on the off chance that anything, developed since 1992 with the extension of the Internet, the truth of psychological oppression, pressures on hydrocarbon powers, the risk of an unnatural weather change, and overall pandemics. Notwithstanding vulnerability, formal planning has additionally experienced harsh criticism for obstructing trust and strengthening, two new ideas in the advancing corporate culture, just as for smothering development.

Chapter 10: So Simple But So Hard

These principle is so easy yet so many people fail to live it out. It's what you KEEP that determines your financial success. PAY YOURSELF FIRST! You may think that it's quite unrealistic to pay yourself first when you have so many other financial obligations. Then again, you should remember that even though it's necessary for you to pay bills and other fees, you also have to plan for your future. You have to be mindful from this day onwards that you need to invest and save at least ten percent of your money. Ideally, you should pay yourself ten percent of your income, then put away this money in a savings account. Do this every month. Set a goal to save 1,000 dollars into an emergency fund as soon as possible. This will help you tremendously if something relatively inconvenient were to happen. Then work on saving between 3-6 months worth of living expenses. Only after that should you start to create a short term and long term savings plan for other material things you want to buy. Saving for retirement is also important in addition to an emergency fund. As an example, even if you only save a hundred dollars per month into a mutual fund that increases ten percent per year, you can have more than a million dollars when you retire if you were to start early enough. It doesn't matter if you only earn a minimum wage. If you save early and long enough, you can be a millionaire. It's not easy to develop a lifelong habit of investing and saving money. You need to exert tremendous willpower and determination. Set a goal and write it down. Then, create a savings plan and do your best to stick with it. Do this over and over until it becomes automatic. Practicing frugality can help you achieve financial success. Evaluate all your expenditures and defer or delay your buying decisions as much as possible. Keep in mind that the longer you put off finalizing a buying decision, the better decision you will have.

How to Develop the Habit of Saving Money?

If you are experiencing difficulty paying yourself first, you can use the following pointers as guidelines: Determine how much you can afford . Take a closer look at your expenses and find out if you can make small changes in your spending habits. For instance, you may choose to bring your own lunch to school or work to save money. You can also cut your cable subscription which can easily cost over 100 hundreds per month. Even a nice alternative like a Neflix subscription is only 10 dollars and with that you can save money and still have some entertainment. These small changes can add up over time and result in a significant difference.

Set personal payment goals . If you know that you cannot afford to pay yourself ten percent of your income right now, make sure to increase your payment the following month. Sometimes, you may need to make adjustments and that's alright, as long as you make up for it as soon as possible. Figure out how much money you should set aside to meet your financial objectives, such as paying for college or going on a vacation. Moreover, see to it that you make changes that can affect your expenses in the long run. Come up with a strategy for saving money . When you find out how much money you have to pay yourself, you have to find a way to save money until you need it. You can begin by opening a savings account and depositing money into it every month. Do this before you pay off your bills. You can either do a direct deposit, so a percentage of your money can directly go into your savings account or set up automatic transfer for your salary every payday. This sends money to your savings account from your checking account, so you can get used to living on a smaller paycheck.

Chapter 11: Setting Your Goal

Budgeting is most effective when it is anchored on a financial goal. The goal that is associated with it should come with a reward.

A person who has accumulated a big debt for instance, could set his budgeting goal to get out of debt. New parents, on the other hand, can set a goal to save for a fund for their new child. You should also set your own goal depending on your own personality and your needs.

Create a goal for each aspect of your life

In reality, a person cannot have just one financial goal. An average person needs to save for a retirement fund, an emergency fund, a fund for buying a home, and probably a car fund. If you wish to start a business, you may also need to set up a fund to serve as the capital. Your budget will help you achieve all the financial goals you set.

You should start by creating a set of goals that you want to achieve in the future. These goals should be important to you. Do not put goals just because you like the idea of achieving them. Instead, you want to be absolutely passionate about these goals. This will ensure that you will be motivated to work on them.

Budgeting requires discipline. If you are not passionate about your financial goals, it is extremely easy to quit on them.

Set your financial priorities

While we all have multiple financial goals, we cannot achieve them all at once. Instead, we need to work for them one at a time. After making a list of financial goals, identify which ones are most important to you.

Some of these goals should be on top of the list by default. A person in debt, for instance, should make it his or her goal to get out of debt first. He or she should prioritize this before going after any other financial goal. The same goes for saving for an emergency fund and for a health care fund.

Other types of financial goals may seem unimportant because the deadline for them is still a few years away. However, for some of these goals, it is necessary to start immediately. Saving for a retirement fund or your child's college fund are prime examples. You need to start saving for them as soon as possible to make use of the effect of compounding interest.

Whichever goal you pick as your topmost priority, it should be the one that you should start working on first. If this goal requires you to save a huge amount, you need to set up a savings account for it.

Write down what you wish to accomplish on a piece of paper and post it somewhere you can see every day. You could also put a copy of this note in your wallet and your credit card sleeve. This way, you will always remember your goal when you are about to spend for something.

Set your target savings rate

Now that you have a goal in mind, it is necessary to identify how much of your income you need to save if you wish to reach your goals on time. You will need to set your savings rate. This is the percentage of your income that you will set aside every month. Every sound budgeting guru suggests that you should save a chunk of your money first before spending any of it. Ideally, you should set the money aside the moment you receive it. This way, you will avoid the temptation of spending most of it and neglecting saving for your goal.

Setting aside your savings before doing any spending will also give you an idea of how much you have left to spend. Whatever is left after you set aside your savings becomes the amount that you need to budget for your daily expenses.

114

To set your savings rate, you will need to identify the timeline and your goal's target amount. Let's say your goal is to save $1,000 in 5 months. This means that you will need to save $200 every month. If you have a $4,000 net monthly income, your savings rate should be at least 5% of your income to reach your goal. Depending on your spending habits, this savings rate could be easy or difficult to reach. To prevent your spending habits from affecting your ability to reach your goal, you need to put away 5% of your income in a separate bank account right after receiving it.

This is only the beginning

It is common for people to only set a budget when they are in a tough financial situation. It is possible that you are reading this book because you are in such a situation. Budgeting though, will only be truly successful if you set it to become a part of your lifestyle. While most people start learning about budgeting as a necessity, they can turn it into a lifelong habit. The people who do this become financially independent and make the most out of their hard-earned cash.

Chapter 12: Identify The Budgeting Roadblocks

Everyone runs intoroadblocks when they try to start budgeting. The sooner you become aware of these roadblocks, the easier it will be for you to overcome or find strategies to work around them. Let's start by identifying your budgeting challenges:

Track your spending

By definition, budgeting is the skill of allocating your funds to control spending. It is only natural to think of your old spending habits to be the primary challenge in implementing any budgeting scheme.

In the first week of putting your budgeting plan to action, you should start tracking your spending. You have a variety of tools to do this. For instance, you can use the old but reliable pen and notebook method. First, you should find a notebook that you can fit in one of your pockets. The idea is to take note of all the things you spend on. Keep it simple by taking note only of the amount and the name of the item or service that you paid for.

If you think of yourself as a forgetful person, you can choose to write down your spending right after you paid for it. If you are good in keeping routines on the other hand, you can take note of your spending every two or three hours, depending on when you take your breaks from work. You could also make it a point to ask for a receipt for all the things you buy. This way, you will be able will have documents to help you remember about all your expenses.

You also have the option of using digital tools. If you have a smartphone, you can use an app to track your spending. There are a lot of great apps to choose from. Some of them allow you to set goals and keep track of your progress in reaching your financial goal. These types of apps can serve as a substitute for the pen and paper method.

Lastly, you will need a tool to help you keep track of your credit card spending. Relying on your credit card for your daily expenses can lead to a financial disaster if you do not know how to use it. There are also some apps that you can use to keep track of all the credit card payments you make. You may also just keep all the receipts that come with your credit card purchases and enter them to a ledger at the end of the week.

Identify bad spending habits

Tracking your spending will allow you to learn about the things that you usually spend on that you can do without. In most cases, people learn about the different vices that they have that eat up a huge chunk of their budget. A smoker, for instance, will realize how much his smoking habit actually costs. A person who is fond of going out with friends will learn how much this lifestyle choice is costing him.

You should also identify which recurring expenses are most costly for you. Most of the time, it is not just one habit that causes a person to overspend but multiple small habits. Make a list of all the spending habits that you can do without. This list will be a crucial tool when creating strategies on how you can improve your budgeting performance.

Your bad spending habits will often become the roadblocks in achieving your financial goals. Budgeting your income will help you prevent this from happening. At the end of your first week of tracking your expenses, review the data you've collected and categorize your expenses according to what type they are. The majority of your expenses are necessary expenses that you cannot do without. Identify the ones that do not fall in this category, and start thinking of ways on how you can prevent them in the future.

Continue keeping track of your expenses using your preferred method. You may need to transfer the data you gather to a tool that can handle a bigger set of data. Ideally, you should use a spreadsheet software for this. You will find that there are many people online offering ways on how to do budgeting using a spreadsheet file as your primary tool.

Compare spending with your income

Aside from allowing you to identify your bad spending habits, tracking your spending also allows you to learn what percentage of your income you usually spend every month. If you rely on your credit card for your everyday expenses, there is a possibility for your spending to actually be bigger than your income. You do not want this to happen.

After you track your spending for a week, compare your total spending to your weekly income. If your spending is close to reaching your income amount, you will be able to save very little from it.

If this is the case, you will need to make major changes on how you spend your money if you want to reach your financial goals. Your budgeting should allow you to set aside the saving rate that you decided on earlier. If possible, you should live with the amount that is left after setting aside your savings.

Chapter 13: The Budgeting Breakdown

Budgeting is the method by which one formulates a framework to expend his money. The framework, which one formulates, is termed as a budget. Framing such an outline to spend your money gives you the scope to adjudge if sufficient money will be there for you to spend on your other objects of interests or on matters of secondary importance.

Once you initiate your budget, you will observe that you might have to align your priorities. There will be certain expenses which you might want to postpone or decline. One of the things you have to be careful about is that you contemplate about various alternate options before expanding your budget. There might be occasions where you will not have any option, for example during an inflation when expenses boom up, in such scenarios simply go for the cheaper or better option that is available before you rather than complying with the high rates.

Does it sound too complicated? Do not worry, budgeting is nothing but ensuing stability between your expenditure and revenue. Not maintaining this stability might lead to more expenditure than revenue. This, will lead to difficult situations. Those who do not make such efforts and expend money than they make, gradually start taking debts. Nobody wants that. These loans only increase over the time until they take charge of their monetary accounts.

In order to effectively master this skill, you need to analyze what the building blocks of good are financing. Most of us do not have sufficient money to execute every desire and idea of ours. It is for people like us that this expense scheme process is meant so that we give precedence to more essential needs.

Why is it so important to budget?

Now you may think why we need to do so much of planning and take up the hassles of pre-planning a budget. Budgeting involves you to pre-plan your expenditures; there is a certainty that there will be a sufficient amount for you to invest in truly important things. Therefore, the fact is that in order to avoid the major hassles in future, we need to take up the minor efforts to budget. The most important aspect of budgeting is that you will not have to take up loans or be indebted to any creditor. It is also your master key to resolve and sort any loan that you are presently indebted with.

How to initiate Budgeting? - The first step towards money management.

The first step for you is to truly comprehend your resources. Your must know and analyze the source of your revenue and how much is the inflow. Obviously, the parallel requirement is to observe and note where your expenses lie, example monthly domestic expenses, your kid's school fees and stationery requirements, amount paid to domestic help and other such helpers etc.

You may want to adapt any of the following methods to note down and track your money.

The Pen and Paper- this is by far the best, easiest and the most convenient method. It is low-tech and handy for all. With a calculator to aid you, you are good to go

A Spreadsheet- for women who prefer digital maintenance of accounts, automatic calculations and a more systematic layout.

Personally, I adhere to the pen and paper. I carry my notepad with me at all places so that I make an entry of even the minutest amount that I spend. Gradually, it became a habit with me and now my hands on their own reach out for my journal to make a quick entry.

You do not have to follow my way though. Nevertheless, in order to track your expenses in the best manner, there is no substitute to religiously making entries of every penny that you spend. A daily analysis and entry of expenses in your page will help you keep a detailed record, without missing out any financial transaction. You may make separate categories for your expenses so that you know better which arena requires more attention and where you need to curb down a bit.

Initiating a systematic budget is a great step to take, however the tricky part is to actually adhering to the budget that you have prepared for your home. You will be startled to see that the tiny expenditures that you incur, sum up to make a large amount. Make sure you slot a time for yourself every week so that you overview your expenditure so far. If you feel that you are going well, it is a good sign but if you feel you are having difficulty in sticking to it, then you might need to reframe it to suit your lifestyle in the long run. Moreover, you might also have to make certain adjustments in your spending habits to accommodate to your budget. A few months into budgeting, and you shall definitely see your family treading the path of greater happiness!

Chapter 14: Setting Financial Goals

Decide to Start a Budget

The first step in creating any kind of change in your life is to make a decision to start. This is an important part of the process because without determination, you will not be able to follow through with your plans. However, deciding to start a budget should not only be done with your words. Shouting, "I have decided to start a budget!" will not make the slightest difference. Instead, putting your words into action will. Which brings us to the next question: How do I act upon my decision?

There are several ways that you can act on it. One of the best ways that you can start with is to gather all the financial data that you will need to create a budget. This includes recent receipts, bills, pay slips and other financial documents. For now, organize them in chronological order and put them in one file.

Another important thing that you should do is to dedicate a part of your time to create a budget. If you have the luxury of time then lucky for you. However, if you are constantly on the go, you have to make a commitment to your decision by sparing a few hours of your time. You can work on creating a budget at least an hour every day or you can spare a weekend to get everything done. Whatever pace works for you just make sure you get it done. Remember, the longer you procrastinate and delay creating your budget, the more money you will be spending mindlessly.

Set a Financial Goal

Every journey must have a destination. Without one, it's not called a journey. It's simply called wandering. The same goes with creating a budget. Without a goal in mind, you won't be able to maintain living on a budget. Without a purpose, maybe a special "reward" to look forward to, it will be easy to fall off the wagon.

Setting a financial goal is a very personal decision. It differs from one person to another and is based on your own needs and desires. Before you start to jot down the numerous goals that you want to achieve, keep in mind that you need to be able to set two kinds of goals: a short-term goal and a long-term goal.

What is a Short-term Goal?

You might think that you don't need a short-term goal because the long-term one is more important. You might even think that it is just another unnecessary expense that you need to cut out of your budget. Do not make the mistake to do so. You are wrong if you think in such a way. A short-term goal proves useful in keeping you motivated to work on your long-term goal.

Imagine going on a six-hour hike and bringing only a limited amount of water.

How will you hydrate yourself? Are you going to drink a particular amount every hour as you hike? Or are you going to "conserve" your water by refraining from drinking any until you reach the summit? Doing the latter will only cause you to collapse in the middle of your hike. The former is the wiser choice for you to reach the top.

This analogy is applicable in explaining the importance of a short-term goal. To set one, ask yourself this question: What do I need or want to buy this month? Unless you have a huge income, stay off high-ticket items or goals that will require you to splurge a lot of money. For example, you only have about $500 left at the end of the month. You can set more than one short-term goal and your short-term goal/s can be as simple as the following:

Deposit $300 in my personal bank account and $200 in the kids'.

Deposit $300 in my personal bank account, spare $150 to buy whatever I want at the mall and keep $50 as money for emergencies.

Deposit $200 in my personal bank account, $200 in the kids' and use the $100 on a simple family outing by the end of the month.

Keep your short-term goal realistic and practical. Do not get carried away by the thought that you can do whatever you want to with your extra-money. Train your mind to be happy with simple things that matter such as the financial security of your family. Having an extra $500 will give you the buying power to purchase an expensive pair of shoes but will it matter?

What is a Long-term Goal?

This is where the big-ticket items and the deepest wishes of your heart go. In figuring out your long-term goal, there is only one question that you need to ask yourself: What do I really need or want in life? To buy a nice home for my family? To avail of a new car? To go on a holiday in

Hawaii? Think of the next three to five years. Think even of the next decades! Whatever your long-term goal, be sure to identify it. In time, it can change as you also adapt to life, but what's important is that you should always have one. Here are examples of long-term goals that might start some ideas brewing inside your own head:

1. Save $400,000 within eight years to buy a house.

2. Save $150,000 within five years for the children's college fund.

3. Save $25,000 within two years to buy a new car.

A manageable way to achieve your long term goals is to divide it into several small goals. Saving $25,000 will be easy enough if you regularly put aside $200 weekly.

As you begin to live on a budget, never forget your purpose for doing so. A good way to remind yourself of the financial goals that you have set is to write it down on your planner or to make a creative reminder like a poster. Putting it in a location where you can always read it (office desktop or bedroom wall), will constantly remind you of the goals that you plan to achieve.

Do not underestimate the power of conditioning. Everything starts in the mind so in order to create a change in the financial aspect of your life, it is best to start the change within your mindset.

Chapter 15: Budgeting Basics And Benefits

What is budgeting? At its most basic, it's just a spending plan you develop based on how much money you make and how much money you spend. Most people make a monthly budget, though if they are especially vigilant with their finances, a weekly one gives them even more control. A budget will be broken up into different categories like "entertainment," "groceries," "utilities," and more, so you can see exactly where your money is going. If you overspend in one category, you can make changes the next month to balance everything out. Depending on what works best, people will use a basic spreadsheet, a mobile app, or even a handwritten system. We'll get into your options in this chapter. There isn't a "right" or "wrong" way to budget; it's about personal preference.

Benefits of budgeting

Why should you take the time and effort to create a budget? Isn't it enough to just watch your spending and make sure all your bills are paid? If you think short-term, that may be sufficient, but life is not a short-term situation. Here are five reasons why everyone should budget:

It lets you plan for your goals

Everyone has life goals they hope will become a reality someday. Maybe you want to buy a house or go on a big trip to Europe. If you don't budget your income accordingly, you'll never have enough money saved to see those dreams come true. Budgeting gives you a concrete goal and provides you with a monthly plan on how to get there. Instead of buying whatever you want when you want it, you now have perimeters you need to stay within in order to reach those long-term goals.

It prevents you from spending money you don't have

Without a budget, it's really easy to end up spending more money than you have. What seems like a small purchase can put you over and if it becomes a habit, those small purchases add up really quickly. Living beyond your means is a really dangerous game. A budget reveals what income you have coming in, so when you divvy up the money on food, utilities, entertainment, and so on, you know where that money goes. You can be sure you aren't spending more than you have access to.

It ensures you are prepared for emergencies

Bad things happen, whether it's illness, car trouble, or a loss of employment. When you have a budget, you can plan for emergencies by saving a portion of your income just for those unpredictable events. When something unexpected does come up, you can use budgeting to adjust your spending habits and move money to where it needs to go. You'll be in control and the emergency won't seem quite as overwhelming, at least financially.

It lets you plan for retirement

Nobody wants to work until they die. Retirement may seem like a far-off dream, depending on your career and age, but it will become a reality one day. If you budget now with retirement in mind, you can avoid needing to get another job when you're 65+ and living a lifestyle that doesn't make you happy. There's a lot that goes into planning for retirement that we won't discuss in this book, but just know that budgeting is a huge part of it. Part of your monthly income should go into retirement-focused categories like your IRA, 401(k), investments, and so on. When you budget with the future in mind, you're setting yourself up for happiness.

It gives you peace of mind

Unless you're a millionaire, money is a stressful thing. The vast majority of people get anxious about bills, unexpected expenses, the future, and so on. Budgeting puts you in the driver's seat of your finances, giving you more control over your money. You won't be in the dark about how much you can spend on groceries to avoid dipping into the red. Depending on your situation, that number might be hard to stick to, but at least you know what the number is. Month-to-month, you'll have a clear picture of the bills that need to be paid, how much they'll cost, and what adjustments you need to make with the other categories. Knowledge is power and peace of mind.

Budgeting styles

We mentioned earlier that there are countless ways to budget, but what are some of the most common and effective? Let's discuss five: the line-item budget, the 50/30/20, the pay-yourself-first, the zero-based, and the cash-only.

The line-item budget

This is the most basic or traditional budgeting style. It's great for people who want to get out of debt, need to control their spending, or who like categorizing expenses. It does take some time and effort, and can be a bit mind-numbing. However, it's also the budget that works the best for most people. You first list all the categories your money goes to each month, both fixed and variable. Fixed expenses are the ones like rent, credit card payments, and insurance. These don't change month-to-month. Variable expenses include groceries, entertainment, and gas. These are different each month.

When creating your budget, you can divide up the categories even more and have individual sections for stuff like groceries, eating out at restaurants, clothing, pet supplies, and so on. Some people like getting really detailed so they can see exactly how much money they're spending on, say, personal care (haircuts, hair products, body wash, razors, etc) each month.

Once you have these categories, you create two columns - one for how much you want to spend and then one for how much you actually spent. This way you can quickly see if you're sticking to your budget, and you can look back as the months go by to see how you're doing overall. If you consistently go over your budget in certain categories, you know it's time to make some changes in your spending habits.

The 50/30/20 budget

A lot of budgeting experts really like this method. It gets its name from the fact that you spend 50% of your month income on needs (bills, food, gas, etc); 30% on wants (movie tickets, books, vacations, etc); and 20% on debt and savings. It's a good style for people who don't want to spend a lot of time working with a line-item budget.

Depending on your financial situation, you can adjust the percentages a bit. If you have a lot of debt, it might be better to follow a 30/10/60 model, so you're aggressively targeting that debt. If you think 30% of your income on needs isn't enough, but you're willing to reduce spending on your wants, just flip the other numbers around so you're following a 50/10/40 budget. If you really want to save money for a goal like buying a house, increasing that last number is also a good idea.

The tricky part about this budgeting method is deciding what it is a "need" and what is a "want." If you're interviewing for a new job, does buying a new suit count as a "need" or a "want," since it will help you make the best impression possible on your potential employers? You've had a really rough time recently with depression, and feel like an overnight trip to a spa with your best friend could give you a powerful emotional boost. Is that a "need" or a "want?" While on the surface, the

50/30/20 budget style is less work than the line-item, you will probably spend a lot of time and energy wrestling with yourself about the "need/want" definition.

The pay-yourself-first budget

With this budgeting style, you focus on saving. As soon as you get paid, you put the money safely away before you spend it on anything. This is a good method for people who having trouble saving, but don't want to spend a lot of time and effort pouring over a detailed budget. It's also a great method for building up an emergency cushion, paying off debt like student loans, and getting closer to your long-term goals like retirement and house ownership. It ensures you always have money when you need it.

The first step is to add up your monthly income and then subtract your monthly expenses. That number is what ends up in your savings. Experts recommend putting at least 5% of your income into savings, so your expenses and spending habits should allow that. If you keep going into the red, you should adjust your spending, and not the number that goes into your savings. Making sure to save least 5% of your income is the top priority with this method. Make adjustments in your monthly expenses to get back into the green. We talk about how to reduce your spending in a later chapter, so hang tight.

The zero-based budget

With this budgeting style, you want every dollar of your income to have a job, and at the end of the month, you haven't spent more. Everything zeroes out, with your money going to pay for expenses or ending up in savings. This is a great style for people who want complete and total control over their money. If you are detail-oriented and a bit of a micromanager, the zero-based budget was designed for you. Be sure to include categories for unexpected costs, or you won't be able to stay at zero at the end of each month. That being said, people who successfully follow this type of budget are able to pay off 19% more debt than others, and save 18% more money.

This budget style does take more effort than others, because it is so numbers-oriented. Before committing, track your expenses for a few months and figure out where your money is going, and how much. This lets you build a realistic framework and figure out where you need to reduce your spending. Once you have this information, you can decide if a zero-based budget is something you want to implement.

The cash-only budget

This last budgeting style is also known as "envelope budgeting." It's basically a simplified version of line-item budgeting. You designate a certain amount of money to a variety of categories, like groceries, entertainment, and so on. However, the big difference is you only use cash. At the beginning the month, you get all the money you'll need in paper form and put it in envelopes for each category. Once it's gone, it's gone. Write down exactly what you spent the money on - you can also keep receipts - and keep the information with their respective envelopes.

If you have trouble with overspending or credit and debit cards, this budgeting style is a great way to get things under control. It isn't easy, but if you really need to get out of debt or stop overspending, it can make a really big difference. You do need to be very careful about those envelopes and keep them in a safe place, so they don't get lost. Certain bills will still need to be paid online, most likely, but whenever you can use cash, use cash.

Chapter 16: How To Make A Budget To Achieve Your Goals?

If you are having a hard time with debt, then creating a budget can be a real help. However, it's important that you create a budget the right way. Many people make the mistake of sitting down, calculating all their expenses and then trying to reduce them by some arbitrary percentage such as 10% or 20%.

Where you should start

The correct place to start in creating a budget is by defining your short and long-term goals. Your short-terms goals should be the ones you can expect to accomplish in a year or so. For example, if you're having a problem with debt, your best short-term goal might be to get rid of it. The point is to pick a goal you can expect to achieve and that you can keep track of on a monthly basis.

Next, define your long-term goal or goals. This could be to buy a house, send your kids to college or to save for a retirement.

Now that you know

Now that you know what your goals are, you'll know how much you will need to save every month and can start creating a budget that will get you there. For the sake of example, a short term goal would be the need to save $200 a month towards getting out of debt and another $100 for a long-term goal of investing for retirement.

Track all of your spending

Your next step will be to track all of your spending for at least 30 days. You can do this the old-fashioned way with a pencil and a notepad, or if you have a smartphone, there are many expense tracking and budgeting apps available. Two of the most popular are Mint (mint.com), and You Need A Budget. I recommend one of the budgeting apps because it will take much of the work of creating and sticking to a budget off of your shoulders. For example, many of them will automatically divide your spending into the appropriate categories - food, entertainment, transportation, insurance, medical expenses and so forth.

When you can see where your money is going

When you can see where your money is going, next comes the important part. You need to figure next out where you can make the cuts required to get your spending down enough below your income that you will be able to save for your goals. Getting back to our example, if your goals require you that you save $300 a month, you will need to cut your spending to at least $300 below your income.

The low hanging fruit

If you and your family are typical consumers, there is some low hanging fruit or areas where you should be able to cut your spending pretty substantially. First and foremost among these is food. This is an area where with a little effort, you should be able to cut your costs by several hundred dollars a month. You can do this by a combination of shopping smart and by the use of coupons and store specials. Second, you may find that you could easily save another $100 a month by reducing the amount you spend on entertainment. Sitting at home, eating a pizza and watching a rented movie might not be as much fun as dining out and then going to a theater but it's a lot cheaper and will save you money.

Chapter 17: Lifestyle Changes To Save Money

Sadly enough, many of us live lifestyles that go way past our means. In a society that offers us money that we haven't earned yet, (aka credit cards and loans) we find that we tend to use resources that we shouldn't in order to live a lifestyle we enjoy. However, we need to take a step back from that way of thinking and think about living our lives with what we do have. What changes can we make to our daily living that will help us save money? Let's take a look!

Find a change in your job or career

If you are underemployed, then that can be one of the first areas that you can change in order to change your financial situation. The fact is, many people take lower paying jobs simply because they feel like they cannot achieve better. If you are one of these people, consider finding a better job or ways to move up in your current place of employment. The more confident you are that you can change your earning situation, the better chances you have of achieving higher pay.

Pick up a side job

If you have time, try having a small part time job that can give you extra income. This income can then be put into the bank and saved for your future use. It may not be possible to carry two jobs, but if you find that you can do so, this is a great way to earn extra income to help your present situation until you start to see an increase in your wealth.

Look for sales

Every place has sales. It's a marketing tool that stores use in order to bring in customers. The great thing about this is that many competitors carry the same products, so looking for sales on the items you need at different stores might help you to save a little extra money. Take some time and look for store ads or on store websites to see the specials that they are currently offering!

Find alternatives to spending

If you're the type of person who likes to go out and spend money, find ways that you can still enjoy your time out without spending. If you like shopping, turn to window shopping. If you like to eat out, budget this into your expenses so that it won't cut into money that you may not necessarily have.

Cut back on things that are not necessary

Current trends in society encourage us to just do whatever we want to do. However, half the time, the money we spend and the time we invest are not worth it. Before you take your time and money to go out on the town, think about whether or not it's really necessary to do so. When confronted with something that you really want but really cannot afford, think about whether or not you really need it. Thinking before we spend our hard earned money can help us steer our financial situation in the right direction.

Live in a place you can afford

Everyone is focused on what you can get when looking for a place to live. However, people are often struggling to make ends meet because they live in places that they really cannot afford. Living in places that are cheaper is not wrong. Once you better your situation, you can always move up into the types of places that you would rather live. Take that into consideration if you struggle financially. Can you get away with living elsewhere while you work on saving money and furthering your employment situation?

Learn to give up unnecessary outings

It feels like people never stay home anymore. Our society encourages us to be out and about almost all the time. However, going places costs money. You have the cost of transportation, tickets, food, or whatever else may come with the outing. Before going out, think about whether or not the outing is necessary. Sometimes we do need to get out, and that's perfectly okay. However, when it becomes a regular and expensive habit, we are cutting into our financial resources and stopping ourselves from enjoying wealth.

Find activities that work with a budget

You might be one of those people who want to do things on a regular basis with your friends or family. Take some time and find activities that won't break you budget. There are tons of fun activities out there for cheap. It's just a matter of finding them and working them into your plans!

Budget your earnings

People may hate the thought of budgeting. However, the most successful and wealthy people in the world live on budgets. By knowing where their money is going and what they can spend, they put limits on themselves. These limits help guide them in making choices that affect their money. If you haven't tried making a budget, maybe you should give it a try. Who knows, it might be the key to gaining your wealth!

Changing spending habits can be difficult, especially if you are in the habit of doing certain activities and purchasing certain items. However, if you look at the big picture, you may realize that what you are currently doing is really not working out in helping you to rise from poverty. I encourage you to take a look at your habits and see if there are any changes you can make in order to save yourself money while still enjoying your life.

Chapter 18: The Principles Of Saving Money

Let this be known: there is no perfect law when it comes to saving money. What exists are a collection of best practices. These practices are a result of success stories told by people who emerged as champions when it comes to frugal living. What they attained is a different level of financial security that is even better than being financially free. Even freedom comes with a price, but when you're secure, you'll survive. Here are some of the principles you can apply as you learn the trade in saving money.

Financial organization

When you organize your finances, you follow an inventory procedure in order to know how much you have (your assets) and how much you can lose (taxation, depreciation, etc.). There are a lot of ways that allows you to save money when you organize your finances. One of which is assessing the tax value of your assets. Find out how much tax applies to your property, your accounts, and so on. When you know how much you'll be charged, you can look for ways to defer it.

On the other hand, financial organization also entails operating within a budget. If you have the ability to track your finances, you'll minimize losses resulting from unnecessary spending. One tool that helps you do that is your monthly budget. If you think that the super rich do not operate within a budget, you're wrong. In fact, a lot of them do because they can potentially lose their wealth with one big mistake. So if they do have a budget, why can't you?

Debt management

Until your debts are paid, you will not really have the monopoly of saving money. In ideal circumstances, you can channel money from your income to increase your savings or to prepare for retirement.

However, in the middle of it all, you have debts to pay. That's why debt management is important, and it should start as early as your first mortgage.

It is true that it is not easy paying loans like mortgage. You know that some mortgage loans take a lifetime to pay. However, realize that that's not the kind of life you wanted to live. One day, you want to see yourself free of any financial obligations. Use this motivation to save money. The rule of thumb is: never pay a debt by getting another debt. Hence, debt management is the best solution. We'll talk more about this in the next chapter.

Spending management

The urge to acquire things is a natural inclination, but it ceases to be natural when we are ruled by impulsive buying. You know that you're an impulse buyer when you feel bad about the thing you purchased, when you feel bad about the act of buying itself, when your budget is destroyed, and when you end up with a money deficit that is proportional to the item you bought.

If you are an impulse buyer, you should distinguish between the items that you need and those that you want. With all things equal, those that you need to should prevail on your list of "To-buys." If that's not the case, realize that you are unnecessarily losing money over things that you would just throw away in the future. You can't throw away your savings account though, can you?

Savings are for future spending

You don't set aside money and let it sit in your bank account. There has to be a reason for your doing so. This reason is the same fuel that makes the act of saving worthwhile and not simply an act of conformity. If you save, be prepared for the day that you will use it on something significant.

In order for you to not exhaust your savings account in a single occasion, try dividing your money into three groups or accounts: one for emergency situations, one for long-term saving, and one for potential investment in the future. If you save money because you have a goal in mind, you'll get more motivated. As you see your money grow, you'll begin to appreciate the renewed power you have over money and not the other way around.

Know the rules about money

You're probably not happy with the thought that you need to revisit the basic laws of Mathematics in order for you to understand how money works. Know that doing so is inevitable because to understand money, you need to know its value both in the accounting part of things, investment, and taxation.

If you familiarize yourself with the rules involving money, you'll know how to invest it and seek ways to optimize your earnings later on. Remember that even traders do not haphazardly place their calls without prior thinking. In the same way, you can't afford to lose money because ignorance is never an excuse.

Saving is not self-deprivation

There's a difference between someone who lives frugally from someone who lives in self-deprivation. Frugal living means that you're still capable of indulging yourself. On the other hand, self-deprivation is denying yourself from experiencing something good. Always remember that you should not deprive yourself so you can tell the world that you have money.

What happens if you deprive yourself? The answer is self-explanatory: you might get sick or you might get depressed. Both situations might prompt you to spend money just the same – a loss that would have been prevented if you allowed yourself to be happy once in a while.

Make money work for you

Originally, money was invented so that people will have an easier medium for trading. Now, it seems as though most people are grappling with the idea on whether or not that still holds true. Apparently, people nowadays are working too hard so they'll have money. On the other hand, there are people who master the laws of money and who make money work for them. The difference is clear, as you can see.

The former situation entails high dependence on money. If it's scarce, those who work for it will suffer. In contrast, those who make money work for them will feel safe during the rainy days because their actions are not limited by money.

Set a financial goal

When you save money, you need to set milestones to mark your accomplishments. That way, you celebrate the little things that move you closer to your ultimate goal. In this case, you should identify a big goal and set smaller goals as stepping stones.

In addition, setting a financial goal also involves looking at the bigger picture. If you know where you wanted to be in the future, you must have a plan on how to get there. In this case, we're talking about financial security.

Again, the laws of money are fluid, and so are the principles involved in it. You are therefore encouraged to use the principles discussed here as a guide only. You'll probably develop your own principles when it comes to saving money. If you can personalize the manner at which you approach saving, go for it. In the next chapter, let's get more specific by discussing one of the greatest challenges in our lives today: debt.

Chapter 19: Identifying Income And Expenses

The very first step in creating a budget is to keep track of your income and expenses. These two are closely related, so you need to carefully monitor any movement. In reality, anyone can make a sound financial plan with any kind of income. All a person has to do is to keep the amount of expenses less than the income, and voila! – They're saving money for their future. For instance, if Mary's income is $5,000 a month and her total expenses for every month only amount to $2,500, Mary can live comfortably and still have some money left for savings and luxuries. However, if Mary's monthly income is only $2,000 yet she has $2,500 in expenses, then there may be a problem! Mary's needs to find a way to bring her expenses down to $2,000 or less, then it would work out. It is helpful to understand therefore that there are two ways for people to maintain a good financial plan. You can either decrease your expenses to fit the income, or increase your income to accommodate all expenses.

With all of that said, it helps to take a close look at your overall income. What kind of income do you have? Do you have a fixed, regular, monthly salary like that of an 8-hour job employee? Or does your monthly income vary based on commission, or the availability of work, like that of a freelancer? Creating a successful budget will also depend on the stability of your income. When you are not sure about how much your income will be each month, it affects your ability to create a sound financial plan. Whether you're an 8-hour-job employee or an independent contractor, you should also make sure to list down as your income only the money that you take home after taxes (this is your "net income"). Don't write down your pre-tax income as that can ruin your budgeting later on.

Identify your expenses and put these in categories that you can easily recognize. Example of these categories would be Food, Utility Bills, Clothing, Auto, Home, Personal, Travel, and so on. It is really up to you to make the categories because it is designed for you to easily identify where your money is going. Once you have created the categories, put under it the items that belong there. For example under Food you can write Groceries, Starbucks, and Eating Out. For Personal you can include Shopping, Fitness, Spa, and Salon and, for the Utilities category, scribble Phone Bills, Internet, Electric, and Water. Break down all your expenses and be as detailed as possible so that you can keep track of every cent that leaves your wallet. If you do this diligently, you won't be wondering later where your money went.

Now that you've written down your overall income and total expenses, try comparing the two. If the result is a negative number then you may be overspending. However, if you still have some money left from your paycheck even after deducting your tax and expenses then you can divide this amount into other categories such as Spending Money, Savings, Retirement Fund, and Emergency Fund.

Although you can always find ways to earn more money, failing to curtail your expenses early on can allow it to build up over time. It is still advisable to cut down on your outflows, whether you plan to increase your income or not. That will help you in creating a budget for you and your household.

Chapter 20: Learn From The People Who Became Very Rich By Saving Money

Being rich, having a lot of money, and being financially free are very trendy topics on which there are countless books. Sure, everyone would like to know the secret with which you can become a millionaire as quick as possible and fulfill all your dreams. Such "tips" on fast wealth may work for the first few in a niche, but unfortunately everyone else usually loses money. You may even have had a bad experience with false promises of quick money.

Saving is an area that most people would like to overlook. It sounds stingy and too strenuous. So why should you choose this book? Because that's what this is all about: getting rich by saving. There are several reasons why it was a good decision that you picked this book and not another one:

1. I live by this philosophy and it works

There are not only collected lists from the Internet in this book, but the savings tips are thoroughly tried and tested. The good thing is that the more the wealth grows, the faster it will become even bigger because you can safely invest some of the savings. At the age of 18, I had 30'000 Fr. in my account. Despite taking driver's ed, studying, and traveling in Australia and the Pacific Islands for 9 months, I had 100'000 Fr. on my savings account when I was 23. At 28, my fortune reached the 350'000 mark. So, I'm on the right track to half a million, and believe me, I'm enjoying my life to its fullest. This takes me to the next point.

2. You'll learn how to save without feeling that you've got to give up everything.

I was a bit of an extreme as a child what concerns money. I have no idea why I was so frugal as a kid because my family was typically middle class. Neither poor nor luxurious, but we had everything we needed and could afford regular holidays. So, there was no reason why I always put most of my pocket money in my piggy bank while my brother was buying sweets with his money. But somehow, I couldn't help it. I always felt that there were even better things to buy and that I wanted enough money to be able to afford them. From 15 to 24, this earned me the nickname bargain hunter, which was not necessarily positive in the eyes of others. When I was 25, I wanted to change something. It couldn't be that I had more money than all my friends, but (except extensive travel) I spent less money than them every month.

Maybe it is difficult for you to understand, but it was very hard for me to start spending more money. I had to force myself to treat myself to more Starbucks coffee or the more expensive pizza if I wanted to.

The great realization was that even though I felt like I had totally gone overboard this month, I was still saving more than I did the previous month. My saved (and invested) money had started to work for me. So, I told my conscience that I could afford more without being scared of going broke and people who newly met me would no longer call me a penny pincher.

I told you this little story of my life so that you understand that I really know how to save properly, but now I have learned that you don't have to give up everything to achieve your savings goals. A good middle way is realistic and will also bring you forward.

3. Saving money is the surest way toward owning a million

Did you know that most millionaires did not get rich through lucky investments, but through constant work and smart saving? The book "**The Millionaire Next Door**" by Dr. Thomas J. Stanley and Dr. William Danko states that the typical millionaire does not show how rich he/she is, because he/she chooses to live in a normal neighborhood and drive average cars. The people who are thought to be super-rich often live above their means and the wealth is short-lived.

This knowledge should now help a pleasant calmness to spread inside you. Because it means that your saved money will not put any pressure on you. You won't have to keep up with any expected standards. You can confidently enjoy your wealth by using it for things that are really important to you (traveling, dining in nice restaurants, or a sports car), but you don't have to prove how much money you have on all levels. While your environment is constantly worried about how they can get to the end of the next month and still afford their Zalando packages or technical innovations, you smile and look at your growing account balance.

*You can double-click on photos to enlarge them

4. Learn how to make the money work for you

Once you've saved your first ten thousand, you can make the money work for you and make even more profit. You don't have any pressure to make the quick buck and it would be a shame to lose a lot of money in the event of a malinvestment. That's why we're going to look at some investment opportunities that will grow your wealth in the long run.

Now you know, why reading this book will benefit you. So, if you're interested in becoming a millionaire, read on and dive into savings tips and the guaranteed growth of your wealth (in no time).

Chapter 21: The Law Of The Vital Few

The Law of the vital few, which is also called Pareto law or the 80/20 law, is a law that states that a minority of efforts, inputs or causes always leads to the majority of rewards, outputs and results.

Basically, it means that 80% of the results that you would get in any given activity you commit yourself to would come from 20% of your inputs.

For instance, in any country, only about 20% of the population own 80% of the wealth available in the country.

In most organizations, 20% of the staff earn 80% of the total salary while the remaining 80% of workers are left to share the remaining 20%.

20% of the nations in the world have 80% of the money in the world while the rest (the remaining 80%) own just 20%.

I could go on and on with practical examples of how the 80/20 law is not just a myth but a reality of life. Even in your personal life, the 80/20 law is evident. You most likely use 20% of your shoes and clothes 80% of the time while the remaining 80% are worn 20% of the time.

So what does this law have to do with financial freedom?

Conventional wisdom teaches you that the most efforts give the most rewards. It teaches you that all inputs are equal and would bring equal results but this is a fallacy. The truth is that only about 20% of the money you get will generate 80% of the wealth you will ever own.

Isn't this surprising considering that you have always thought that the more money you earn, the richer you would become. Of course, more income is good but only about 20% of that extra income would generate wealth for you.

All your income is considered as 100%. The 80% portion goes is used to settle your bills, feed yourself, cloth yourself, secure accommodation and provide comfort for your family. The remaining 20% is a seed. Although it seems like a very small portion of your income, when you consistently set it aside and invest it wisely, it would be your gateway to financial freedom.

I know you probably know that to be financially free, you must learn how to save and invest your savings. But for you to get there, it is necessary that you appreciate the fact that for you to save, you must budget. Without a budget, anything goes and the likelihood of you having any surplus is pretty slim. Let's learn about budgeting in the next chapter.

Conclusion

Thank you again for purchasing this book on budgeting your personal finances!

I am extremely excited to pass this information along to you, and I am so happy that you now have read and can hopefully implement these strategies going forward.

I hope this book was able to help you understand how to better manage your financial life and helps you to accomplish your goals. Also, if you know of anyone else that could benefit from the information presented here please alert them of this book.

The next step is to get started using this information and to hopefully live a happier, healthier and much more fulfilling life!

Thank you and good luck!